FAMILY

Also by
SHARON SLOAN FIFFER AND STEVE FIFFER

*Home: American Writers
Remember Rooms of Their Own*

*Fifty Ways to Help Your Community:
A Handbook for Change*

FAMILY

*American Writers
Remember Their Own*

EDITED BY
SHARON SLOAN FIFFER
AND STEVE FIFFER

AFTERWORD BY JANE SMILEY

PANTHEON BOOKS   NEW YORK

The following essays were previously published:

"To the Point: Truths Only Essays Can Tell" by Edward
Hoagland, in *Harper's Magazine,* March 1993 · "The
Faintest Echo of Our Language" by Chang-rae Lee, in
the *New England Review,* Summer 1993 · "Heavy Lifting"
by Geoffrey Wolff, in the *San Diego Reader*

Library of Congress Cataloging-in-Publication Data

Family: American writers remember their own /
edited by Sharon Sloan Fiffer and Steve Fiffer;
afterword by Jane Smiley.
p.   cm.
ISBN 0-679-44247-2
1. Authors, American—20th century—Family relationships.
2. Family—United States.   I. Fiffer, Sharon Sloan, 1951–   .
II. Fiffer, Steve.
PS129.F27   1996
810.9'0054—dc20   96-14359
[B]   CIP

Random House Web Address: http://www.randomhouse.com/

Book design by M. Kristen Bearse

Printed in the United States of America
First Edition
2 4 6 8 9 7 5 3 1

CONTENTS

INTRODUCTION:

SKELETONS

SHARON SLOAN FIFFER

My dad was good with numbers. He liked counting, fingering coins, shuffling bills, and adding up long columns of figures. In high school, when I'd run in for breakfast, late, out of breath and pulling up my dark green regulation knee socks, I almost always found Dad at the kitchen table, counting up the change from the jukebox or the cigarette machine. Sometimes he'd have a few coins set aside, a buffalo nickel, a silver dime, a steel penny. "They're valuable," he'd say, smiling at me, "hang on to them."

My dad and mom owned and operated the E Z Way Inn in Kankakee, Illinois. The building itself was a tumbledown box, with shingled siding and a tar paper roof, but its success could be measured by the real estate tenet—location, location, location. Directly across from 2228 West Station Street was the Roper Stove Factory, previously the Florence Stove Fac-

Aunt Jessie holding Donald

tory, previously the E Z Way Stove Factory. When the E Z Way Inn was first tacked together, it was practically the company store.

Although Mom made soup and sandwiches for the factory workers, it wasn't a restaurant or even a café. Yes, there was a kitchen, an eight-burner stove with an enormous grill, cast-iron skillets the size of a small country. There were even sandwich specials of the day—roast beef on Monday, cubed steak on Tuesday, bar-b-que on Wednesday, Polish sausage on Thursday, and if it's tuna salad, it must be Friday. A walk-in cooler was attached to the back of the ramshackle building. Formerly a refrigerated train car, it now held cases of Bud and Blatz and Schlitz and Pabst right next to my mom's kettles of vegetable soup and gallon containers of mustard, mayo, and pickles. But despite the gourmet menu and four-star restaurant equipment, it was a tavern or, as my dad preferred, a saloon. He liked to call himself a saloon keeper.

Once, ready for school early, I found my dad at the kitchen table pondering an envelope with numbers written all over it. The change and bills from yesterday's business were already in cigar boxes, and Dad already had his coat on, and his brimmed tweed hat was pushed back a little on his forehead. His pipe was next to the ashtray, but he was smoking a cigarette. I poured cereal into a bowl and he whispered, "There are 1,440 minutes in a day."

"Yeah?"

"That's 365 days in a year."

I stopped pouring and listened.

"I've been alive 19,465 days. That's 28,129,600 minutes."

"What's the point of this, Dad?" I had a Latin test first period, my bangs were sticking straight out, and now my dad was getting spooky on me.

"Or 1,681,776,000 seconds."

"Dad?"

"It's just something to think about." He smiled and passed me the milk.

My dad was fifty-three years old then. I was fourteen. I didn't get it.

Later that same year, my dad decided I was old enough to be confused even more. He told me the family secret, the secret that belonged to his mother, my Grandma Henry.

Grandma Henry was bitter, but not insane. It's true that when I knew her best, she lived at the Kankakee State Hospital in a cavernous stone dormitory called Hampton Hall, but she was employed there as a seamstress, not committed as a crazy. She taught the patients how to sew. Her classroom was a large high-ceilinged room filled with long tables and outdated sewing machines. Grandma always isolated me from the patients on my weekend visits, but one time a woman walked into the room and came right up to my face, stared deep into my eyes, and introduced herself, shaking my hand for a long time. Months later, when I was spending a Friday night sleeping over at Hampton Hall with Grandma, she handed me a rag doll. It was tightly sewn together, neat stitches and well-turned corners. The face, though, was off center. One eye was larger than the other and a corner of the mouth drooped. The patient I had met made it and asked Grandma to give it to me. "I was going to throw it away," my grandma said, "but sitting under that lamp on my dresser, it looked sort of sweet." Grandma pursed her lips tightly, then relaxed them. "Now I've given it to you, you can do what you want with it."

My grandma was a devout Republican. She demanded clean fingernails, shined shoes, and good manners. She taught me to embroider, turning over my work and inspecting the wrong side as closely as the right side. "It's the underside that shows if you're good with a needle," she'd say, ripping out a row of x's and handing me a newly threaded needle so I could try again.

Every Christmas season, Grandma Henry took my brother and me to Chicago on the train. First, we went to Bramson's to pick up the underwear she special-ordered twice a year, then to Marshall Field's to see the giant Christmas tree and pick out a toy, then to a Cantonese restaurant on Wabash, where we ate chop suey and chow mein, drank tea, and read our fortunes out of cookies.

So here's the secret. My grandma gave her baby away.

Jessie Schmidt Henry, my father's mother, was widowed for the first time in 1918. My grandfather, Emory, was due to begin service in World War I on Monday, but died from the flu on Friday. Grandma herself was ill and not expected to live. Her mother, my great-grandmother, tended to her and asked, "Jessie, what will you do? Emory is dead. What will you do?" My grandma was too sick to answer or even to have her children near. My father, Donald, six, his sister, Maxine, four, and the baby, Richard, two years old, were kept away.

There is no one alive who can tell me what words were said, what promises were made. But somehow, between the fever and the recovery, my grandmother had agreed to give up her baby, Richard, to be adopted by her childless older brother, John, and his wife, Dorothy. It was to remain a secret. Richard would call his uncle and aunt, John and Dorothy, father and mother. Jessie, my grandma, if she lived, would become Richard's aunt. Those were the rules.

Grandma Henry did live. She used her husband's life insurance to put herself through business school. She had a head for figures, learned bookkeeping, and kept accounts for Volkmann's, the fanciest jewelry store in Kankakee. There, she met an older man, a man the age of her father. She married him, confident, I am sure, that he would take care of her and her two children. I like to think she nourished a hope that with money, with this older man's money, she could reclaim her youngest child. But the old man lost all his money in the Depression and my grandma and her two children, almost grown, were poorer than they had been before. When Mr. Henry died, my dad and his sister were already adults, on their own, so my grandma went to work at the State Hospital.

Every summer, Grandma Henry took two vacations. One was a real trip, on a train, to California to see her daughter, Maxine, and her family. She took my brother with her when he was twelve, and when I turned eight, she took me. Two days and nights on the El Capitan from Joliet, Illinois, to San Bernardino, California.

The second vacation was a trip to central Ohio. My father would drive her to see her brother and sister-in-law and their son, Richard. When they returned, my grandmother would sit stone-faced at our window. "Did you have a nice time, Grandma?" I always asked. And she would stare through me, and say, "If only he wouldn't call me Aunt Jessie. It's the way he says 'Aunt Jessie.' " I asked what she meant and she'd wave me away, tears in her eyes. I would hug her and bring her the makings of my latest project, a square yard of one-inch pink-and-white checked gingham. She had promised to teach me to smock. Pulling herself together, she'd wipe her eyes and watch me gather in the corners of the small pink squares. I was eight years old and knew it was my job to make my grandma feel better, to keep her busy.

When I was older, fourteen, a freshman in high school, I no longer made aprons or embroidered dish towels. I knew then what my grandma had done. As she sat brooding by the window after her annual Ohio visit, I could think of nothing to say to make her feel better. I couldn't reconcile my stern but loving sewing teacher with a mother who could give up her baby boy. I was old enough to know the family secret, but I still had a teenager's heart, all soft sentiment, little hard compassion. I didn't get it. It didn't add up.

Grandma is gone. She died in California, cared for by my aunt Maxine. My dad died at sixty-eight of lung cancer. During one of his last stays in the hospital, his brother/cousin Richard came to visit. He stood by my father's bed with his hand on my father's hand.

"Everybody who caused all the trouble, all the pain, everybody who kept all the secrets is dead. We don't have to keep their secrets, Don."

I tiptoed out of the room and they talked. I think they cried. I know I did. My uncle Richard, whom I was seeing for the first time, looked exactly like my father. A few inches shorter, but it was the same face. They even wore the same style of glasses. My uncle had children, three or four, and they were my first cousins. I remember thinking that they might look just like me.

I fantasize about meeting them, recognizing them while on a family vacation—you know, while I'm pointing out Mount Rushmore to my son, I look up and see another mother, my exact double, pointing out Jefferson's nose to her little girl. Perhaps it's because I prefer the romance of fantasy or the drama of surprise that I've never actually written a letter or made a call to set up a meeting. Or maybe it's fear of being the messenger. What if they don't know the secret?

I asked my dad before he died if he remembered calculating with pen and paper the minutes and seconds he had lived. If he by any chance remembered that morning when I was fourteen, the year I was trusted with the family secret. He shook his head. I told him that I didn't get it then, but now I realized he was teaching me to reflect and to meditate. He was advising me that life was complicated, full of intricate twists and turns. He was cautioning me to take nothing for granted, to waste not even one second of my life. He shook his head and smiled. "Honey, I just liked to do multiplication."

Open any closet. You will find a family secret. Perhaps not one that rattles its bones, and sends you to Ohio searching for brown-eyed cousins with a prominent overbite, mirror images who will look at you across a bin of finishing nails in an unfamiliar hardware store and ask, "Do I know you?" Perhaps your secret will tell you why the smell of garlic makes you hear your mother's song or why a row of brown bottles on a shelf sends you off to phone your cousin. Open any door and find family. Those whose blood is the same as yours, those you've married, those you've lost, those you've found, those you've chosen.

Open this book, any chapter. Turn any page and find your family.

FAMILY

Lillie Lulkin

ALICE HOFFMAN

When crossing the street, never trust the judgment of drivers. They may not stop for you. They may roll over you, and keep on going. In fact, never trust anyone. They're not your family, their blood is not half as thick as water, why would you take their advice? Do they have your best interest at heart? Not one bit, and frankly, neither do most of your own relatives. It's dog eat dog, it really is, although what can you expect? Life is hard. Life is a battle. Life is what you make of it. Be prepared with a career. Retail is good—people are always buying. Everything could be burning down around them, and they're buying. You can call this sort of behavior foolish, but it's human nature. It's hope.

. . .

All people are created equal—black, white, Chinese, Moroccan, it doesn't matter. Equal. Everyone. All the same, whenever there's a murder, check the newspaper to make sure the culprit isn't Jewish—you'll breathe easier if you do. Then double-check and make sure the murderer isn't from New York—you'll breathe easier still. Give to charity, but don't tell your relatives that you do. Keep secrets well. Don't lie, but never tell the whole truth. That sort of thing is too hard to swallow, honey. That's what fiction is for.

Anything served in a fancy restaurant can be equaled in your own kitchen. As a matter of fact, everything can be made out of potatoes—bread, soup, pancakes, cake. Alone on a desert island, all a person really needs is a bag of potatoes and a toaster oven. Forget planes, jets, cars, TV. Without a doubt, a toaster oven is the finest invention of the twentieth century. It broils, it bakes, it toasts, it sits on your counter, small as a mouse. Always read labels. What? You're surprised it's so full of chemicals? You think these companies have your best interest at heart? But a potato. There's nothing evil they can do to it. No additives or red dye or msg there. A potato is a hundred percent pure. It is what it is. Unlike most things.

Between men and women, love is not only blind, but stupid. Oh, sure, love has a sense of humor, but the punch line is usually sex, money, despair, or kids, and none of these are particularly funny. Here's how you test if love is real. Broil a chicken (with a side dish of potatoes, naturally) and invite him over.

Cook badly. Even if you're already a bad cook, make it worse. Trust me, it's easy. Throw in anything you want. Too much salt, too much pepper. Feed him and see what he says. A complaint means he's thinking about himself, and always will. A compliment means he'll never make a living. But a man who says "Let's go to a restaurant," now he's a real man. Order expensive, and see what he's got to say then. Kiss him good-night. Go ahead, don't be afraid. Do you hear your blood in your head moving too fast? Are you faint? Do you need a Tylenol? Are you sick to your stomach and shaky in your knees? That's love all right, so don't fight it, honey, because in such matters, no human is immune. Not even you.

Don't kid yourself—nothing lasts forever. This can be both a plus and a minus. A plus if you buy on credit and drop dead before payments are complete. A minus if you purchase an item, a horse, for instance, or a washing machine, and it either dies or breaks down and there you are, still paying out monthly installments. This philosophy can be applied to marriage and to life in all its forms. When something doesn't last forever, you can wail and moan or thank your lucky stars. After all, would you rather be stuck with a bill for a dead horse or cheat the seller from your grave?

Sleep is overrated. Who needs it? Do you know how much you could accomplish while all those idiots out there are asleep? You could be first in your class, you could write twenty novels, you could polish your furniture, which I notice you've never before considered. And, after all, it's true that with sleep come dreams. Sometimes when I wake up I look in the mirror and expect to see a girl of sixteen, and I'm shocked by the stranger looking back at me. I dream about my mother, who made a sour-cherry pie that was so delicious people said angels must have been beside her in the kitchen. Don't ever do what I did and throw caution to the wind. Don't marry for love. The one I picked, when I fixed the chicken and potato dinner to test him, he simply pushed his plate away. He was so lovesick he didn't eat! I should have seen him for who he was. I should have known that this kind of man would wind up sleeping on sunny afternoons, stretched out on the couch, and that the smile on his face would be so sweet no woman with half a heart would dare to wake him.

Try it and you'll see I'm right. If you stay awake, you'll hear the cockroaches and be ready for them with some spray or a shoe. You'll be prepared to throw a book at those mice who think they're so smart as they run along your counter. You'll see the morning star and the way the sky looks like heaven when it's still so early daytime itself seems like a dream.

Wear an apron when you cook. Put on heels when you go out to dinner. Buy your cemetery plot with a group—you get a better deal that way. Stay in school. Don't eat pork. Don't even look a pig in the eye, or you'll get dizzy. Always go to at least two doctors when you're sick, so you get a second opinion, and when you're given a prescription, only take half. They always want to overdose you, and half is plenty. Usually, a scarf around the neck, tea and lemon and whiskey will cure anything. For a broken heart, eat ice cream. For your wooden furniture, olive oil, plain and simple, and it doesn't have all those lousy chemicals they're always pushing off on us.

Women can do anything men can do and more, but is this any reason to tell men the true story? Let them think what they think. Do they believe the proper use of a screwdriver means a higher intelligence level? Fine, if they do, let them. Good luck to them. When you have a baby you will know a secret that no man can ever know. You may forget it later, but for a little while you will know that within yourself you hold another's life. This puts the ability to use a screwdriver in its proper place. Nowhere. Unless you've got furniture you need to put together.

If you ever lose a child, the way I did, then you'll know the other side of the truth. You'll understand what it means to be destroyed and still get up every day and fill the kettle with water. You will see steam from the kettle and weep. Insist nothing is wrong. A piece of dirt flew up and lodged beneath your eyelid. That's all. On the street, tears will fall onto the sidewalk and fill up your shoes. Say the sun is in your eye. Maybe you have pink-eye. If you show your grief, it won't go away. If you keep it se-cret, it won't go away. It is with you forever and ever, but there may be an hour when you don't remember. An evening when the sky is blue as ink. An afternoon when your daughter runs after a cricket she will never catch. Whisper your baby's name. Then be quiet. If you're lucky you'll hear the name said back to you every time you close your eyes.

. . .

Always accept apologies. It won't hurt you to be gracious, and no one knows what you're really thinking, inside your head. Wear black for all occasions, including weddings, bar mitzvahs, and funerals. When I die, bury me quickly. Don't be afraid to leave me in the ground. I'm not frightened, and I never have been. Not about those sorts of matters. Wear low shoes on most occasions and a warm coat. Don't be so snotty about putting on a pair of gloves in cold weather or taking food home from restaurants. Why do you think doggie bags were invented? When you have a rent-controlled apartment to sublease, give it to a relative.

Don't think that good deeds go unforgotten. Don't think that is the point of good deeds. Some people believe that the more you do for others, the quicker your spirit flies, or the better you sleep at night, which is fine if you believe in such things.

Bathing on a cold day is worse for your health than a little dirt will ever be. Spit on the ground when you hear gossip, so you can listen in peace without fear of slander seeking you out. Stay away from spiders. Wash your face with oatmeal. Take long walks, but not after dusk. Once, when I was little, I went where I wasn't supposed to go at twilight and saw a rabbit grabbed up by a great big bird, a hawk, it may have been, or an owl. There were feathers on the ground. There was blood everywhere. I stood watching, in my one good dress that was blue as my father's eyes, and I thought I did not want to be the rabbit or the owl. I wanted to be the sky they had both disappeared into. I wanted to never give up.

. . .

Being old is not what you think it is. You feel the same. You are the same. The woman beside you is the girl she once was. Remember that. Remember me.

LILLIE LULKIN
1903-1987

Brent Staples, age nine months, at the Patterson family farm in Hollins, Virginia. Summer 1952.

BRENT STAPLES

The mother at the beach was supernaturally pale, speaking that blunt Canadian French with a couple on the next blanket. At the market, she wore a business suit and was lost in a dream at the cheese counter. At the museum, the mother was tan and grimly thin, wearing ink-black shades and hissing furiously into a pocket phone. I was watching when each of these women let a small child wander away. The events were years and cities apart, but basically the same each time. I shadowed the child and waited for its absence to hit home. A mother who loses her cub—even for a moment—displays a seizure of panic unique to itself. Those seizures of panic are a specialty of mine. I guess you could say I collect them.

This morning I am walking to the doctor's office, brooding about mortality and the yearly finger up the butt. Today's mother has flaming red hair and is standing on the steps, riffling her bag for keys. Her little girl is no more than four—with the same creamy face, trimmed in ringlets of red. The mother's hair is thick and shoulder length, blocking her view as she leans over the bag. The child drifts down the steps and stands on the sidewalk. Idling as children do, she crosses to the curb and stares dreamily into traffic. Three people pass her without breaking stride. A pair of teenagers with backpacks. A homeless man pushing a junk-laden shopping cart. A businessman, who glances up at the woman's legs and marches onward.

For some people a four-year-old beyond its mother's reach is invisible. For me that child is the axis of the world. Should I run to her, pull her back from the curb? Should I yell in crude Brooklynese, "Hey lady, look out for the friggin' kid!" Nearing the child, I croon in sweet falsetto, "Hey honey, let's wait for Mommy before you cross." The mention of Mommy freezes her. Up on the steps, the red mane of hair whips hysterically into the air. "Patty, get back here! I told you: Don't go near the street!" The woman thanks me and flushes with embarrassment. I smile—"No trouble at all"—and continue on my way.

Most men past forty dream of muscle tone and sex with exotic strangers. Mine is a constant fantasy of rescue, with a sobbing child as the star. What I tell now is how this came to be.

My parents were children when they married. She was eighteen. He was twenty-two. The ceremony was performed in the log house where my mother was born and where she, my grandmother Mae, and my great-grandmother Luella still lived, in the foothills of the Blue Ridge Mountains. I visited the house often as a small child. The only surviving picture shows a bewildered toddler sitting in the grass, staring fixedly at an unknown something in the distance. My great-grandmother Luella was a tall, raw-boned woman with a mane of hair so long she had to move it aside to sit down. Her daughter, my Grandma Mae, wore tight dresses that showed off her bosoms and a string of dead foxes that trailed from her shoulder. The beady eyes of the foxes were frightening when she bent to kiss me.

The log house had no running water, no electricity. At night I bathed in a metal washtub set near the big, wood-burning stove. Once washed, I got into my white dressing gown and prepared for the trip to the outhouse. My grandmother held a hurricane lamp out of the back door to light the way. The path was long and dark and went past the cornfield where all the monsters were. I could tell they were there, hidden behind the first row, by the way the corn squeaked and rustled as I passed. Most feared among them were the snakes that turned themselves into hoops and rolled after you at tremendous speed, thrashing through the corn as they came.

The outhouse itself was dank and musty. While sitting on the toilet I tried as much as possible to keep the lamp in view through cracks in the outhouse wall. The trip back to the log house was always the worst; the monsters gathered in the corn to ambush me, their groaning, growling reaching a crescendo as they prepared to spring. I ran for the light and landed in the kitchen panting and out of breath.

My father's clan, the Staples of Troutville, had an indoor toilet. My paternal great-grandparents, John Wesley and Eliza Staples, were people of substance in the Roanoke valley. In the 1920s, when folks still went about on horseback, John Wesley burst on the scene in a Model T Ford with all the extras—and let it be known that he paid for the car in cash. Though not an educated man, he could read and write. He was vain of his writing: he scribbled even grocery lists with flourish, pausing often to lick the pencil point. There was no school for black children at that time. And so John Wesley and his two immediate neighbors built one at the intersection of their three properties. Then they retained the teacher who worked in it.

The Pattersons were rich in love, but otherwise broke. This made my mother's marriage to a Staples man seem a fine idea. But domestic stability was not my father's experience, the role of husband and father not one that he could play. His own father, John Wesley's son Marshall, had routinely disappeared on payday and reappeared drunk and broke several days later. He abandoned the family at the start of the Depression, leaving Grandma Ada with four children in hand and one—my father—on the way. Ada had no choice but to place her children with relatives and go north, looking for work.

The luckiest of my uncles landed with John Wesley and Eliza. My father came to rest in hell on earth: the home of Ada's father, Tom Perdue. Three wives preceded Tom into the grave and the family lore was that he worked them to death. He hired out his sons for farmwork and collected their pay, leaving them with nothing. My father was beaten for wetting the bed and forced to sleep on a pallet under the kitchen sink. He left school at third grade and became part of Tom's dark enterprise. Birthdays went by unnoted. Christmas meant a new pair of work boots—if that. Had it not been for my father and a younger cousin, Tom would have died with no one to note his passing.

This childhood left its mark. My father distrusted affection and what there was of it he pushed away. He looked suspicious

when you hugged or kissed him—as though doubting that affection was real. The faculty for praising us was dead in him. I
could choose any number of examples from childhood, but per-
mit me to skip ahead to college. I was obsessed with achievement and made the dean's list nearly every semester. My father
was mute on the subject—and never once said "good job." Finally, I achieved the perfect semester—an A in every subject—
with still not a word from him. Years later, I found that he had
carried my grades in his wallet and bragged on them to strangers
at truck stops.

My father worked as a truck driver; he earned a handsome
salary, then tried to drink it up. My mother mishandled what was
left. How could she do otherwise when money was a mystery to
her? She grew up in a barter economy, where one farmer's milk
bought another's eggs and the man who butchered the hogs was
paid in port. She stared at dollar bills as though awaiting divine
instruction on how to spend them.

I grew up in a household on the verge of collapse, the threat
of eviction ever present, the utilities subject to cutoff at any moment. Gas was cheap and therefore easy to regain. The water
company had pity on us and relented when we made even token
efforts to pay. But the electric company had no heart to harden.
We lived in darkness for weeks at a time. While our neighbors'
houses were blazing with light, we ate, played, and bathed in the
sepia glow of hurricane lamps. My mother made the darkness
into a game. Each night before bed, she assembled us in a circle
on the floor, with a hurricane lamp at the center. First she told
a story, then had each of us tell one. Those too young to tell stories sang songs. I looked forward to the circle and my brothers'
and sisters' faces in the lamplight. The stories I told were the first
stirrings of the writer in me.

On Saturday night my father raged through the house hurling things at the walls. Sunday morning would find him placid, freshly shaven, and in his favorite chair, the air around him singing with Mennon Speed Stick and Old Spice Cologne. At his feet were stacked the Sunday papers, *The Philadelphia Bulletin* and *The Philadelphia Inquirer.* I craved his attention but I was wary of him; it was never clear who he would be.

On a table nearby was a picture of him when he was in the navy and not yet twenty years old. He was wearing dress whites, with his cap tilted snappily back on his head, his hand raised in a salute. He smiled a rich expansive smile that spread to every corner of his face. A hardness had undermined the smile and limited its radius. His lips—full and fleshy in the picture—were tense and narrow by comparison. The picture showed a carefree boy—free of terrible Tom—on the verge of a life filled with possibility. Ten years later those possibilities had all been exhausted. He was knee-deep in children, married to a woman he no longer loved but lacked the courage to leave. The children were coming fast. We were three, then five, then nine.

Our first neighborhood was called The Hill, a perfect place for a young mother with a large family and an unreliable husband. The men went to work at the shipyard and brought home hefty paychecks that easily supported an entire household. The women stayed home to watch and dote on the children. Not just their own, but all of us. Many of these women were no happier than my mother. They had husbands who beat them; husbands who took lovers within full view of their neighbors; husbands who drove them crazy in any number of ways. The women submerged their suffering in love for children. There was no traffic to speak of, and we played for hours in the streets. A child five years old

passed easily from its mother's arms into the arms of the neighborhood. Eyes were on us at every moment. We'd be playing with
broken glass when a voice rang out from nowhere: "Y'all stop that
and play nice!" We'd be transfixed by the sight of wet cement, ripe
for writing curse words, when the voice rang out again: "Y'all get
away from that cement. Mr. Prince paid good money to have that
done!" Women on errands patroled the sidewalks and made them
unsafe for fighting. Every woman had license to discipline a child
caught in the wrong. We feigned the deepest remorse, hopeful
that the report would not reach our mothers.

Everyone on The Hill grew some kind of fruit; my gang was
obsessed with stealing it. We prowled hungrily at people's fences,
eyeing their apples, pears, and especially their peaches. We were
crazed to get at them, even when they were tiny and bitter and
green. We turned surly when there was no fruit at all. Then we
raided gardens where people grew trumpet flowers, which gave
a sweet nectar when you sucked them. The flowers were enormous and bright orange. When the raid was finished, the ground
would be covered with them.

I lost The Hill when my family was evicted. We landed miles
away in the Polish West End. The Poles and Ukrainians had once
ruled much of the city. They had surrendered it street by street
and were now confined to the westernmost neighborhood, their
backs pressed to the city limits.

My family had crossed the color line. The people who lived
in the house before us had been black as well. But they were all
adults. After them, my brothers and sisters must have seemed an
invading army.

The Polish and Ukrainian kids spelled their names exotically
and ate unpronounceable foods. They were Catholics and on

certain Wednesdays wore ashes on their foreheads. On Fridays they were forbidden to eat meat. When you walked by their churches you caught a glimpse of a priest swinging incense at the end of a chain. I wanted to know all there was to know about them. That I was their neighbor entitled me to it.

The Polish and Ukrainian boys did not agree. The first week was a series of fights, one after another. They despised us, as did their parents and grandparents. I gave up trying to know them and played alone. Deprived of friends, I retreated into comic books. My favorite hero was the Silver Surfer, bald and naked to his silver skin, riding a surfboard made of the same silver stuff. The comic's most perfect panels showed the seamless silver body flashing through space on the board. No words; just the long view of the Surfer hurtling past planets and stars.

My fantasies of escape centered on airplanes; I was drunk with the idea of flying. At home, I labored over model planes until the glue made me dizzy. At school, I made planes out of notebook paper and crammed them into my pockets and books. I was obsessed with movies about aerial aces and studied them carefully, prepping for the acehood that I'd been born to and that was destined to be mine. I planned to join the air force when I graduated from high school. The generals would already have heard of me; my jet would be warming up on the runway.

My favorite plane was a wooden Spitfire with British Air Force markings and a propeller powered by a rubber band. I was flying it one day when it landed in the yard of a Ukrainian boy whose nose I had bloodied. His grandfather was gardening when the plane touched down on the neatly kept lawn. He seized the plane, sputtered at me in Ukrainian, and disappeared into the house. A few minutes later one of his older grandsons delivered what was left of it. The old man had destroyed it with malevolent purpose. The wings and fuselage were broken the long way, twice. The pieces were the width of popsicle sticks and wrapped in the rubber band. This was the deepest cruelty I had known.

My mother suffered too. She missed her friends on The Hill, but we were too far west for them to reach us easily. She was learning how difficult it was to care for us on her own, especially since there were few safe places to play. The new house sat on a truck route. Forty-foot semis thundered by, spewing smoke and rattling windows. My mother lived in terror of the traffic and forbade us to roller-skate even on the sidewalk. On The Hill, she had swept off on errands confident that we would be fine. In the Polish West End, she herded us into the house and told us to stay there until she got back.

The house had become a prison. My eldest sister, Yvonne, was thirteen years old—and the first to escape. She stayed out later and later and finally disappeared for days at a time. My mother strapped her. My father threatened her with the juvenile home. But Yvonne met their anger with steeliness. When they questioned her she went dumb and stared into space. I knew the look from prisoner-of-war movies; do your worst, it said, I will tell you nothing. She lied casually and with great skill. But I was an expert listener, determined to break the code. The lie had a strained lightness, the quality of cotton candy. I recognized that sound when she said, "Mom, I'll be right back, I'm going out to the store." I followed her. She passed the store and started across town just as I thought she would. I trotted after her, firing questions. "Where do you think you're going? What is on your mind? What are you trying to do to yourself?" I was my mother's son and accepted all she told me about the dangers of the night. Girls became sluts at night. Boys got into fights and went to jail. These hazards meant nothing to Yvonne; she ignored me and walked on. I yelled "Slut! Street dog!" She lunged at me, but I dodged out of reach. "Slut" I had gotten from my mother. But "street dog" was an original; I'd made it up on the spur of the moment. I had become the child parent. I could scold and insult—but I was too young and ill-formed to instruct. I relished the role; it licensed me to be judge and disparage people I envied but lacked the courage to imitate.

Yvonne was wild to get away. You turned your back and—POOF!—she was gone. Finally she stayed away for days that stretched into weeks and then months. There was no sign or word of her. My mother was beaten up with worry. By night she walked the floors, tilting at every sound in the street.

What is it like to be one of nine children, to be tangled in arms and legs in bed and at the dinner table? My brothers and sisters were part of my skin; you only notice your skin when something goes wrong with it. My youngest brother, Blake, got infections that dulled his hearing and closed his ears to the size of pinholes. Bruce broke his arm—while playing in the safety of our treeless and boring backyard. Sherri began to sleepwalk, once leaping down a flight of stairs. Every illness and injury and visit to the hospital involved me. I was first assistant mother now, auxiliary parent in every emergency.

My five-year-old sister Christi was burned nearly to death. Her robe caught fire at the kitchen stove. I was upstairs in my room when it happened. First I heard the scream. Then came thunder of feet below me, and soon after the sound of the ambulance. The doctors did the best they could and gave the rest up to God.

The sign at the nurses' station said that no one under sixteen could visit. I was only eleven; with Yvonne missing, I was as close to sixteen as the children got. I knew that Christi had been brought back from the dead. What I saw the first day added mightily to that awareness. A domed frame had been built over the bed to keep the sheets from touching the burns. Peering under the dome, I saw her wrapped in gauze, round and round the torso, round and round each leg, like a mummy. Blood seeped through the bandages where the burns were deepest. The burns that I could see outside the bandages didn't look too bad. The skin was blackened, but bearable.

Eventually she was allowed to sit up. I would arrive to find her in her bright white gauze suit, sitting in a child's rocking chair. I got used to the gauze. Then they took it off to air out the wounds. Her body was raw from the breast to below the knee. The flesh was wet and bloody in places; I could see the blood pulsing beneath what had been her skin. The room wobbled, but I kept smiling and tried to be natural. I walked in a wide circle around her that day, afraid that I would brush against her. I got past even this, because Christi smiled interminably. The nerve endings were dead and she felt nothing. In time I grew accustomed to flesh without skin.

Christi's injuries were the worst on the ward. Next to the burns everything else was easy to look at. I was especially interested in the boy with the steel rods jutting out of his leg. He'd been hit by a car, and the bone was shattered. He didn't talk much, but the rods in his legs were fascinating. The skin clung to them like icing to the candles on a cake.

The children's ward was sparsely visited on weekdays. I cruised the room, cooing at toddlers and making jokes with frightened newcomers. On weekends the ward filled up with parents, highlighting the fact that I was eleven years old—and that my own parents were elsewhere. When real parents visited, I felt like a fraud. I clung to Christi's bedside and did not stray. I wished that the scene at Christi's bed was like the scene around the other beds: fathers, mothers, relatives. But that was not to be.

Christi's accident made the world dangerous. When left in charge, I gathered the children in the living room and imprisoned them there. Trips to the bathroom were timed and by permission only. Now and then I imagined the smell of gas and trotted into the kitchen to check the stove. I avoided looking out of windows for fear of daydreaming. Staring at the sky, I punched through it into space and roamed the galaxy with my hero, the Silver Surfer.

I was daydreaming one day when my brother Brian cried out in pain. He had taken a pee and gotten his foreskin snarled in his zipper. He had given a good yank, too, and pulled it nearly halfway up. Every step tugged at the zipper and caused him to scream. I cut off the pants and left just the zipper behind. To keep his mind off his troubles and kill time until my parents got home, I plunked out a tune on the piano. The longer they stayed away the more crazed I became.

The days were too full for an eleven-year-old who needed desperately to dream. The coal-fired boiler that heated our house was part of the reason. The fire went out at night, which meant that I built a new fire in the morning: chop kindling; haul ashes; shovel coal. Then it was up from the basement, to iron shirts, polish shoes, make sandwiches, and pack the school lunches. My mother tried to sweeten the jobs by describing them as "little": "Build a little fire to throw the chill off of the house." But there was no such thing as a "little" fire. Every fire required the same backbreaking work. Chop kindling. Chop wood. Shovel coal. Haul ashes. One morning she said, "Put a little polish on the toe of your brother's shoes." I dipped the applicator into the liquid polish and dabbed the tiniest spot on the top of each shoe. Yvonne's departure had left my mother brittle and on the edge of violence. I knew this but couldn't stop myself. She was making breakfast when I presented her with the shoes, which were still scuffed and unpolished. "I told you to polish those shoes," she said. "No, you didn't," I said, "you said 'put a little polish on the toe.'" She snapped at me. I snapped back. Then she lifted the serving platter and smashed it across my head.

My father was drinking more than ever. Debt mounted in the customary pattern. We pushed credit to the limit at one store, then abandoned the bills and moved on to the next. Mine was the face of the family's debt. I romanced the shop owners into giving us food and coal on time, then tiptoed past their windows to put the bite on the next guy. When gas and electricity were cut off, I traveled across town to plead with the utility companies. The account executives were mainly women with soft spots for little boys. I conned them, knowing we would never pay. We were behind in the rent and would soon be evicted. Once settled elsewhere, we would apply for gas and electricity under a fictitious name.

The only way to get time to myself was to steal it. During the summer, I got up early, dressed with the stealth of a burglar, and tiptoed out of the house. The idea was to get in a full day's play unencumbered by errands or housework. Most days I escaped. On other days my mother's radar was just too good, and her rich contralto came soaring out of the bedroom. "Brent, make sure you're back here in time to . . ." to go shopping, to visit Christi at the hospital, to go a thousand places on a thousand errands.

Inevitably I thought of running away—to Florida. In Florida you could sleep outside, live on fruit from the orange groves, and never have to work. I decided to do it on a snowy Saturday at the start of a blizzard. Thought and impulse were one: I took an orange from the fruit bowl, grabbed my parka from the coat rack, and ran from the house.

I did not get to Florida. In my haste, I had grabbed the coat belonging to my younger brother Brian. It was the same color as mine but too small even to zip up. The freight train I planned to take never left the rail yard. The snow thickened and I began to freeze. Numb and disheartened, I headed home.

Five years later I succeeded in running away—this time to college. Widener University was two miles from where my family lived. For all that I visited them, two miles could have been two thousand. I lived at school year round—through holidays, semester breaks, and right through the summer. Alone in bed for the first time, I recognized how crowded my life had been. I enjoyed the campus most when it was deserted. I wandered the dormitory drinking in the space. At night I sat in the stadium, smoking pot and studying the constellations. I never slept with my brothers again.

Years later youngest sister, Yvette, accused me of abandoning the family. But the past is never really past; what we have lived is who we are. I am still the frightened ten-year-old tending babies and waiting for my parents. The sight of a child on its own excludes everything else from view. No reading. No idle conversation. No pretending not to see. I follow and watch and intervene because I have no choice. When next you see a child beyond its mother's reach, scan the crowd for me. I am there, watching you watch the child.

Inja Lee

CHANG-RAE LEE

My mother died on a bare January morning in our family room, the room all of us favored. She died upon the floor-bed I had made up for her, on the old twin mattress from the basement that I slept on during my childhood. She died with her husband kneeling like a penitent boy at her ear, her daughter tightly grasping the soles of her feet, and her son vacantly kissing the narrow, brittle fingers of her hand. She died with her best friend weeping quietly above her, and with her doctor unmoving and silent. She died with no accompaniment of music or poetry or prayer. She died with her eyes and mouth open. She died blind and speechless. She died, as I knew she would, hearing the faintest echo of our language at the last moment of her mind.

That, I think, must be the most ardent of moments.

I keep considering it, her almost-ending time, ruminating the nameless, impossible mood of its ground, toiling over it like some desperate topographer whose final charge is to survey only the very earth beneath his own shifting feet. It is an improbable task. But I am continually traveling through that terrible province, into its dark region where I see again and again the strangely vast scene of her demise.

I see.

Here before me (as I now enter my narrative moment), the dying-room, our family room. It has changed all of a sudden— it is as if there has been a shift in its proportion, the scale horribly off. The room seems to open up too fast, as though the walls were shrinking back and giving way to the wood flooring that seems to unfurl before us like runaway carpet. And there, perched on this crest somehow high above us, her body so flat and quiet in the bed, so resident, so immovable, caught beneath the somber light of these unwinking lamps, deep among the rolls of thick blankets, her furniture pushed to the walls without scheme, crowded in by the medicines, syringes, clear tubing, machines, shot through with the full false hopes of the living and the fearsome calls of the dead, my mother resides at an unfathomable center where the time of my family will commence once again.

No one is speaking. Except for the babble of her machines the will of silence reigns in this house. There is no sound, no word or noise, that we might offer up to fill this place. She sleeps for a period, then reveals her live eyes. For twelve or eighteen hours we have watched her like this, our legs and feet deadened from our squatting, going numb with tired blood. We sometimes move fitfully about, sighing and breathing low, but no one strays too far. The living room seems too far, the upstairs impossible.

There is nothing, nothing at all outside of the house. I think perhaps it is snowing but it is already night and there is nothing left but this room and its light and its life.

People are here earlier (when?), a group from the church, the minister and some others. I leave her only then, going through the hallway to the kitchen. They say prayers and sing hymns. I do not know the high Korean words (I do not know many at all), and the music of their songs does not comfort me. Their one broad voice seems to be calling, beckoning something, bared in some kind of sad invitation. It is an acknowledgment. These people, some of them complete strangers, have come in from the outside to sing and pray over my mother, their overcoats still bearing the chill of the world.

I am glad when they are finished. They seem to sing too loud; I think they are hurting her ears—at least, disturbing her fragile state. I keep thinking, as if in her mind: *I'm finally going to get my sleep, my sleep after all this raw and painful waking, but I'm not meant to have it. But sing, sing.*

When the singers finally leave the room and quickly put on their coats I see that the minister's wife has tears in her eyes: so it is that clear. She looks at me; she wants to say something to me but I can see from her stunted expression that the words will not come. Though I wanted them earlier to cease I know already how quiet and empty it will feel when they are gone. But we are all close together now in the foyer, touching hands and hugging each other, our faces flushed, not talking but assenting to what we know, moving our lips in a silent, communal speech. For what we know, at least individually, is still unutterable, dwelling peacefully in the next room as the unnameable, lying there and waiting beside her, and yet the feeling among us is somehow so formidable and full of hope, and I think if I could hear our thoughts going round the room they would speak like the distant report of ten thousand monks droning the song of the long life of the earth.

Long, long life. Sure life. It had always seemed that way with us, with our square family of four, our destiny clear to me and my sister when we would sometimes speak of ourselves, not unlucky like those friends of ours whose families were wracked with ruinous divorce or drinking or disease—we were untouched, maybe untouchable, we'd been safe so far in our isolation in this country, in the country of our own house smelling so thickly of crushed garlic and seaweed and red chili pepper, as if that piquant wreath of scent from our mother's kitchen protected us and our house, kept at bay the persistent ghosts of the land who seemed to visit everyone else.

Of course, we weren't perfectly happy or healthy. Eunei and I were sometimes trouble to my parents, we were a little lazy and spoiled (myself more than my sister), we didn't study hard enough in school (though we always received the highest marks), we chose questionable friends, some from broken families, and my father, who worked fourteen-hour days as a young psychiatrist, already suffered from mild hypertension and high cholesterol.

If something happened to him, my mother would warn me, if he were to die, we'd lose everything and have to move back to Korea, where the living was hard and crowded and where all young men spent long years in the military. Besides, our family in Korea—the whole rest of it still there (for we were the lone emigrees)—so longed for us, missed us terribly, and the one day each year when we phoned they would plead for our return. What we could do, my mother said, to aid our father and his struggle in this country, was to relieve his worry over us, release him from that awful burden through our own hard work, which would give him ease of mind and help him not to die.

My mother's given name was Inja, although I never once called her that, nor ever heard my sister or even my father address her so. I knew from a young age that her name was Japanese in style and origin, from the time of Japan's military occupation of Korea, and I've wondered since why she chose never to change it to an authentic Korean name, why her mother or father didn't change the names of all their daughters after the liberation. My mother often showed open enmity for the Japanese, her face seeming to ash over when she spoke of her memories, that picture of the platoon of lean-faced soldiers burning books and scrolls in the center of her village still aglow in my head (but from her or where else I don't know), and how they tried to erase what was Korean by criminalizing the home language and history by shipping slave labor, draftees, and young Korean women back to Japan and its other Pacific colonies. How they taught her to speak in Japanese. And as she would speak of her childhood, of the pretty, stern-lipped girl (that I only now see in tattered rust-edged photos) who could only whisper to her sisters in the midnight safety of their house the Korean words folding inside her all day like mortal secrets, I felt the same burning, troubling lode of utter pride and utter shame still jabbing at the sweet belly of her life, that awful gem, about who she was and where her mother tongue and her land had gone.

She worried all the time that I was losing my Korean. When I was in my teens, she'd get attacks of despair and urgency and say she was going to send me back to Korea for the next few summers to learn the language again. What she didn't know was that it had been whole years since I had lost the language, had left it somewhere for good, perhaps from the time I won a prize in the first grade for reading the most books in my class. I must have read fifty books. She had helped me then, pushed me to read and then read more to exhaustion until I fell asleep, because she warned me that if I didn't learn English I wouldn't be any-body and couldn't really live here like a true American. *Look at me,* she'd say, offering herself as a sad example, *look how hard it is for me to shop for food or speak to your teachers, look how shameful I am, how embarrassing.*

Her words frightened me. But I was so proud of myself and my prolific reading, particularly since the whole year before in kindergarten I could barely speak a word of English. I simply lis-tened. We played mostly anyway, or drew pictures. When the class sang songs I'd hum along with the melody and silently mouth the strange and difficult words. My best friend was an-other boy in the class who also knew no English, a boy named Tommy. He was Japanese. Of course, we couldn't speak to each other but it didn't matter; somehow we found a way to com-municate through gestures and funny faces and laughter, and we became friends. I think we both sensed we were the smartest kids in the class. We'd sit off by ourselves with this one Ameri-can girl who liked us best and play house around a wooden toy oven. I've forgotten her name. She'd hug us when we "came home from work," her two mute husbands, and she would sit us down at the little table and work a pan at the stove and bring it over and feed us. We pretended to eat her food until we were full and then she'd pull the two of us sheepish and cackling over to the shaggy remnants of carpet that she'd laid down, and we'd all go to sleep, the girl nestled snuggly between Tommy and me, hotly whispering in our ears the tones of a night music she must have heard echoing through her own house.

Later that year, after a parents' visiting day at school, my mother told me that Tommy and his family were moving away. I didn't know how she'd found that out, but we went to his house one day, and Tommy and his mother greeted us at the door. They had already begun packing, and there were neatly stacked boxes and piles of newspapers pushed to a corner of their living room. Tommy immediately led me outside to his swing set and we horsed about for an hour before coming back in, and I looked at my mother and Tommy's mother sitting upright and formally in the living room, a tea set and plate of rice cookies between them on the coffee table. The two of them weren't really talking, more smiling and waiting for us. And then from Tommy's room, full of toys, I began to hear a conversation, half of it in profoundly broken English, the other half in what must have been Japanese, at once breathy and staccato, my mother's version of it in such shreds and remnants that the odd sounds she made seemed to hurt her throat as they were called up. After we said good-bye and drove away in the car, I thought she seemed quiet and sad for me, and so I felt sadder still, though now I think that it was she who was moved and saddened by the visit, perhaps by her own act. For the momentary sake of her only son and his departing friend, she was willing to endure those two tongues of her shame, one present, one past. Language, sacrifice, the story never ends.

Inside our house (wherever it was, for we moved several times when I was young) she was strong and decisive and proud; even my father deferred to her in most matters, and when he didn't it seemed that she'd arranged it that way. Her commandments were stiff, direct. When I didn't listen to her, I understood that the disagreement was my burden, my problem. But outside, in the land of always-talking strangers and other Americans, my mother would lower her steadfast eyes, she'd grow mute, even her supremely solemn and sometimes severe face would dwindle with uncertainty; I would have to speak to a mechanic for her, I had to call the school myself when I was sick, I would write out notes to neighbors, the postman, the paper carrier. Do the work of voice. Negotiate *us,* with this here, now. I remember often fuming because of it, this one of the recurring pangs of my adolescence, feeling frustrated with her inabilities, her misplacement, and when she asked me one morning to call up the bank for her I told her I wouldn't do it and suggested that she needed "to practice" the language anyway.

Gracious god. I wished right then for her to slap me. She didn't. Couldn't. She wanted to scream something, I could tell, but bit down on her lip as she did and hurried upstairs to my parents' bedroom, where I knew she found none of this trouble with her words. There she could not fail, nor could I. In that land, her words sang for her, they did good work, they pleaded for my life, shouted entreaties, ecstasies, they could draw blood if they wanted, and they could offer grace, and they could kiss.

But now—and I think, *right now* (I am discovering several present tenses)—she is barely conscious, silent.

Her eyes are very small and black. They are only half-opened. I cannot call up their former kind shade of brown. Not because I am forgetting, but because it is impossible to remember. I think I cannot remember the first thing about her. I am not amnesiac because despite all this *I know everything about her.* But the memories are like words I cannot call up, the hidden vocabularies of our life together. I cannot remember, as I will in a later narrative time, her bright red woolen dress with the looming black buttons that rub knobbly and rough against my infant face; I cannot remember, as I will soon dream it, the way her dark clean hair falls on me like a cloak when she lifts me from the ground; I cannot remember—if I could ever truly forget—the look of those soft Korean words as they play on her face when she speaks to me of honor and respect and devotion.

This is a maddening state, maybe even horrifying, mostly because I think I must do anything but reside in this very place and time and moment, that to be able to remember her now— something of her, anything—would be to forget the present collection of memories, this inexorable gathering of future remembrances. I want to disband this accumulation, break it apart before its bonds become forever certain.

She wears only a striped pajama top. Her catheter tube snakes out from between the top buttons. We know she is slipping away, going fast now, so someone, not me, disconnects the line to her food and water. The tube is in her way. These last moments will not depend on it. Her line to the morphine, though, is kept open and clear and running.

This comforts me. I have always feared her pain and I will to the end. Before she received the automatic pump that gives her a regular dosage of the drug, I would shoot her with a needle at least five times a day.

For some reason I wish I could do it now:

I will have turned her over gently. She will moan. Every movement except the one mimicking death is painful. I fit the narrow white syringe with a small needle, twisting it on tight. I then pull off the needle's protective plastic sheath. (Once, I will accidentally jab myself deep in the ring finger and while I hold gauze to the bloody wound she begins to cry. I am more careful after that.) Now I fill the syringe to the prescribed line, and then I go several lines past it; I always give her a little more than what the doctors tell us, and she knows of this transgression, my little gift to her, to myself. I say I am ready and then she lifts her hips so I can pull down her underwear to reveal her buttocks.

I know her body. The cancer in her stomach is draining her, hungrily sucking the life out of her, but the liquid food she gets through the tube has so many calories that it bloats her, giving her figure the appearance of a young girl who likes sweets too well. Her rump is full, fleshy, almost healthy-looking except for the hundreds of needlemarks. There is almost no space left. I do not think it strange anymore that I see her naked like this. Even the sight of her pubic hair, darkly coursing out from under her, is now, if anything, of a certain more universal reminiscence, a kind of metonymic reminder that not long before she was truly in the world, one of its own, a woman, fully alive, historical, a mother, a bearer of life.

I feel around for unseeable bruises until I find a spot we can both agree on.

"Are you ready?" I say. "I'm going to poke."

"*Gu-rhaeh,*" she answers, which, in this context, means some cross between "That's right" and "Go ahead, damn it."

I jab and she sucks in air between her teeth, wincing.

"*Ay, ah-po.*" It hurts.

"A lot?" I ask, pulling the needle out as straight as I can, to avoid bruising her. We have the same exchange each time; but each time there arises a renewed urgency, and then I know I know nothing of her pains.

I never dreamed of them. Imagined them. I remember writing short stories in high school with narrators or chief characters of unidentified race and ethnicity. Of course this meant they were white, everything in my stories was some kind of white, though I always avoided physical descriptions of them or passages on their lineage and they always had cryptic first names like Garlo or Kram.

Mostly, though, they were figures who (I thought) could appear in an *authentic* short story, *belong* to one, and no reader would notice anything amiss in them, as if they'd inhabited forever those visionary landscapes of tales and telling, where a snow still falls faintly and faintly falls over all of Joyce's Ireland, that great muting descent, all over Hemingway's Spain, and Cheever's Suburbia, and Bellow's City of Big Shoulders.

I was to breach that various land, become its finest citizen and furiously speak its dialects. And it was only with one story that I wrote back then, in which the character is still unidentified but his *mother* is Asian (maybe even Korean), that a cleaving happened. That the land broke open at my feet. At the end of the story, the protagonist returns to his parents' home after a long journey; he is ill, feverish, and his mother tends to him, offers him cool drink, compresses, and she doesn't care where he's been in the strange wide country. They do not speak; she simply knows that he is home.

. . .

Now I dab the pinpoint of blood. I'm trying to be careful.

"*Gaen-cha-na,*" she says. *It is fine.*

"Do you need anything?"

"*Ggah,*" she says, flitting her hand, "*kul suh.*" *Go, go and write.*

"What do you want? Anything, anything."

"*In-jeh na jal-leh.*" *Now I want to sleep.*

"Okay, sleep. Rest. What?"

"*Boep-bo.*" *Kiss.*

"Kiss."

Kiss.

This will be our language always. To me she speaks in a child's Korean, and for her I speak that same child's English. We use only the simplest words. I think it strange that throughout this dire period we necessarily speak like this. Neither of us has ever grown up or out of this language; by virtue of speech I am forever her perfect little boy, she my eternal righteous guide. We are locked in a time. I love her, and I cannot grow up. And if all mothers and sons converse this way I think the communication must remain for the most part unconscious; for us, however, this speaking is everything we possess. And although I wonder if our union is handicapped by it I see also the minute discoveries in the mining of the words. I will say to her as naturally as I can— as I could speak only years before as a child—*I love you, Mother,* and then this thing will happen, the diction will take us back, bridge this moment with the others, remake this time so full and real. And in our life together, our strange language is the bridge and all that surrounds it; language is the brook streaming through it; it is the mossy stones, the bank, the blooming canopy above, the ceaseless sound, the sky. It is the last earthly thing we have.

My mother, no longer connected to her machine, lies on the bed on the floor. Over the last few hours she suffers brief fits and spasms as if she is chilled. She stirs when we try to cover her with the blanket. She kicks her legs to get it off. Something in her desires to be liberated. Finally we take it away. Let her be, we think. And now, too, you can begin to hear the indelicate sound of her breathing; it is audible, strangely demonstrative. Her breath resonates in this house, begins its final cadence. She sounds as though she were inhaling and exhaling for the very first time. Her body shudders with that breath. My sister tries to comfort her by stroking her arms. My mother groans something unintelligible, though strangely I say to myself for her, *Leave me alone, all of you. I am dying. At last I am dying.* But then I stroke her too. She keeps shuddering, but it is right.

What am I thinking? Yes. It is that clear. The closer she slips away, down into the core of her being, what I think of as an origin, a once-starting point, the more her body begins to protest the happening, to try to hold down, as I am, the burgeoning, blooming truth of the moment.

For we think we know how this moment will be. Each of us in this room has been elaborating upon it from the very moment we gained knowledge of her illness. This is the way it comes to me, but I think we have written, each of us, the somber epic novel of her death. It has taken two and one-half years and we are all nearly done. I do not exactly know of the others' endings.

Eunei, my sister (if I may take this liberty), perhaps envisioning her mother gently falling asleep, never really leaving us, simply dreams of us and her life for the rest of ever. I like that one.

My father, a physician, may write that he finally saves her, that he spreads his hands on her belly where the cancer is mighty and lifts it out from her with one ultimate, sovereign effort. Sometimes (and this ought not be attributed to him) I think that his entire life has come down to this struggle against the palpable fear growing inside of his wife. And after she dies, he will cry out in a register I have never heard from his throat as he pounds his hand on the hardwood above her colorless head, *"Eeh-guh-moy-yah? Eeh-guh-moy-yah?" What is this? What is this?* It—the cancer, the fear—spites him, mocks him, this doctor who is afraid of blood. It—this cancer, this happening, this time—is the shape of our tragedy, the cruel sculpture of our life and family.

In the ending to my own story, my mother and I are alone. We are always alone. And one thing is certain; she needs to say something only to me. That is why I am there. Then she speaks to me, secretly. What she says exactly is unclear; it is enough, somehow, that she and I are together, alone, apart from everything else, while we share this as yet unborn and momentary speech. The words are neither in Korean nor in English, languages which in the end we cannot understand. I hear her anyway. But now we can smile and weep and laugh. We can say good-bye to each other. We can kiss, unflinching, on our mouths.

Then she asks if I might carry her to the window that she might see the new blossoms of our cherry tree. I lift her. She is amazingly light, barely there, barely physical, and while I hold her up she reaches around my neck and leans her head against my shoulder. I walk with her to the window and then turn so that she faces the tree. I gaze longingly at it myself, marveling at the gaudy flowers, and then I turn back upon her face, where the light is shining, and I can see that her eyes have now shut, and she is gone.

But here in this room we are not alone. I think she is probably glad for this, as am I. Her breathing, the doctor says, is becoming labored. He kneels and listens to her heart. "I think we should be ready," he says. "Your mother is close." He steps back. He is a good doctor, a good friend. I think he can see the whole picture of the time. And I think about what he is saying: *Your mother is close.* Yes. Close to us, close to life, close to death. She is close to everything, I think; she is attaining an irrevocable nearness of being, a proximity to everything that has been spoken or written or thought, in every land and language on earth. How did we get to this place? Why are we here in this room, assembled as we are, as if arrayed in some ancient haunted painting whose grave semblance must be known in every mind and heart of man?

I count a full five between her breaths. The color is leaving her face. The mask is forming. Her hand in mine is cold, already dead. I think it is now that I must speak to her. I understand that I am not here to listen; that must be for another narrative. I am not here to bear her in my arms toward bright windows. I am not here to be strong. I am not here to exchange good-byes. I am not here to recount old stories. I am not here to acknowledge the dead.

I am here to speak. Say the words. Her nearness has delivered me to this moment, an ever-lengthening moment between her breaths, that I might finally speak the words turning inward, for the first time, in my own beginning and lonely language: Do not be afraid. It is all right, so do not be afraid. You are not really alone. You may die, but you will have been heard. Keep speaking—it is real. You have a voice.

EDWIDGE DANTICAT

It is a cold Saturday morning, 4:00 A.M. My father gets up to go work. He drives what is called a Gypsy cab. He has been getting up early on Saturday mornings for the last fifteen years.

"Are you warm enough?" my mother asks with sleep in her voice. "Be careful. Stay alert."

They part in front of my room, my father leaving for his car and my mother going back into their bedroom where she watches him from the window as he sits in the front seat and waits for his engine to warm up.

My father has eczema. He has dark sores all over his body that won't heal. They used to be dime-sized and dark, now they are quarter-sized and raw because he scratches them.

I once took him to a well-respected dermatologist on Park

André Danticat

Avenue. Papi thought he had cancer. The doctor performed a biopsy. It wasn't. I then thought that if he drank enough water or used enough skin lotion, the sores would go away, as if he had an extreme case of dry skin, overly dehydrated from the inside.

For years before, my father had gone to doctors in our neighborhood, the ones who charge fifty dollars a visit whether you have insurance or not. In the Park Avenue office Papi felt out of place. There was a very tall model there and a plump girl with braces and bad acne. Papi read his Bible while we waited. When the doctor called him, he was not sure whether to get up or not. He asked me to go into the examining room with him. The doctor let me stay. I saw her chip off a piece of one of the sores, taking one sample from his leg and another from his stomach. When he had to take off all his clothes, the doctor asked me to leave.

Later, my father would ask the doctor why she took no skin samples from the front of his scalp, where all his hair has been falling out. He doesn't know what to make of that. None of the men in his family have ever lost their hair. My father hates losing his hair, or he hates the way he's losing it—slowly. On the way home from the doctor's office, he wondered how his face would look if he had no hair at all on his head.

"Big," I said.

So my father leaves for work that Saturday and every Saturday at 4:00 A.M. There is a lot of business at 4:00 A.M. on Saturday mornings. People are getting out of nightclubs, going home. "At that hour you can get some real drunks," he says.

Once, working on a Saturday morning, my father cut in

front of some young guys in a blue van and they shot three bullets at his car. He had a passenger in the back. "I went so fast, red light after red light, until the passenger was safe."

He never tells us those stories directly unless there is some grave evidence, some obvious mark of what happened. When that's the case, he recounts the events at the Monday night prayer meetings, where people take turns going to one another's houses every week. "Even my family has not heard this," he begins. "I didn't want to worry them. But I need to testify to God's greatness so I won't keep it to myself."

There were also two other incidents that my father couldn't keep secret. Three men he had driven to a far-off area in Brooklyn asked him for all his money when he got there. When they found that he had only a few dollars in his pocket, they hit his face with a crowbar and ran away. His face was bruised and swollen, but given the circumstances, he made out okay. No bones were broken. He was in the hospital only a few hours, most of the time waiting for a doctor to see him.

Another time a man followed him home in a car. My brother André happened to be sitting on the stoop in front of our house and saw this man walking toward my father with his hands buried in his pocket. My father spotted André and shouted, "Call the police." André wanted to keep an eye on Papi, so he walked up to the man. In a more assured voice than my father's, André threatened to call the police and the man walked away.

"This was the first time I'd ever seen Papi scared," André told me and my other two brothers later that day.

I wondered how many of these kinds of incidents have taken place in my father's life over the fifteen years he's been a cab driver. The Park Avenue specialist says that eczema is like your mental state boiling out on your skin. My father always talks about dying. He's sixty years old.

My father was born in a mountain village in Haiti called Beauséjour, which means "a good stay." Recently the Haitian government asked that archivists no longer demand that parents choose between qualifying their children either as *sitwayins*/citizens or *péyizans*/peasants. I was in the car with my father going somewhere when I happened to read this. I asked him about it. He told me that on his birth certificate, it was said he was a *péyizan*.

I don't know very much about the years between my father's birth and his becoming my "Papi." I have gathered only a few patches of information into a small collage, which I have made into my father's past. Our last name was not "Danticat" before my father's generation. If we were to trace our family back beyond my grandfather, we'd have to use the true family name, which was Osnac. As was sometimes the custom in the old Beauséjour, my father's brothers and sisters took their father's middle name, Dantica, as their last name. My father was the first Danticat with a *t,* which was carelessly added on his immigration papers when he applied for a visa to come to the United States.

My father moved from Beauséjour to Port-au-Prince when he was twenty-five years old. He worked as a tailor and then a shoe salesman in a store run by an Italian man in Port-au-Prince. Neither he nor my mother will ever say how they met. I don't think they themselves remember. But they will say that they had a long-distance courtship and that at first Papi's family objected because they had someone else in mind for him to marry. But after he met my mother, every weekend when he wasn't working, he went to a small town in Léogane, a few miles from the city, where he pestered my mother until she married him.

I was born five years after my parents wed. For some reason my mother could not conceive until that time, even though they both very much wanted to have a child. Many uncles and aunts have told me that Papi was overjoyed when I was born: He had wanted a girl. A year later my brother André was born. And then in 1971, when I was two years old, my father moved to Brooklyn.

There, my father lived with his brother-in-law, my uncle Justin, and worked two jobs. One of those jobs was in a car wash during the day, where "even in the cold you had to get wet." The other job was in a sweatshop glass factory that "gave you some idea what hell was like." My father made less than a dollar per hour at each job. He remembers when the price of subway tokens went from thirty-five to fifty cents because the glass factory gave him a penny raise. The car wash job paid for his expenses in the United States. The glass factory job paid for our rent and food in Haiti. In two years, Papi had gathered and saved enough money to pay for my mother's passage to the United States, so he sent for her. But because of immigration restrictions, André and I were not able to come along. We stayed with my uncle Joseph and aunt Denise in Haiti. We were separated from our parents for eight years.

My uncle Joseph and aunt Denise very much believed in "spare the rod, spoil the child." Whenever I misbehaved, they would spank me and spank me good. My brother André was sickly and often bedridden, so he never got spanked as much as I did. I recall getting tired of being spanked one day and shouting, "This misery won't last forever. Wait until my father sends for me." I knew that it was my father who had the power to send for people because he had sent for my mother. My protests against spankings were always answered by a threat from my uncle. "Wait until you go to your Papi; he won't put up with that fresh mouth." Slowly, I grew afraid of my father.

My parents visited us in Haiti in 1976. They brought with them a restless toddler (my brother Kelly) and a sweet adorable baby (my youngest brother Karl). My father, who had a smooth face before, had now grown a beard. I remember the beard prickling my face as he said hello to me and crooned, "Look at my girl, look how big she's become." You leave somebody long enough, they're bound to get big, I thought. I yanked myself away from my father. He felt too much like a stranger and I knew he was not going to stay.

In the two weeks they were in Haiti, when my father called to me, I wouldn't come. When he wanted to play, I ran away. Later, my mother—who I went to and played with—would say, "The way you acted scared your father so much. He knew he had to do all he could to send for you kids. Otherwise, we would lose you."

Because of immigration red tape, it took another five years for my parents to show that they could support us and thus be allowed to have us join them in the United States. In 1981, at the airport in New York, my father was cautious before approaching me. He still remembered my reluctance to go near him when he was in Haiti, and he did not want to be rejected again. He let my mother and my brothers say hello first.

"How was the trip?" my mother asked, as she nudged me toward my father and urged me to kiss him.

At that time I remember thinking, Yes! He's my father all right, because just like me he knows how to hold a grudge.

After we'd just arrived, my father stopped working in the factories and began driving a Gypsy cab. He started driving the cab because he wanted to keep an eye on my brothers and me during the day—which wasn't possible when he was working in the factory.

In the mornings, Papi would take us all to school. My brothers Kelly and André were in elementary school. I was in junior high school, and the youngest, Karl, was in pre-kindergarten.

After he dropped us off, Papi would go to work picking up passengers, and then a few hours later he would collect us all from school.

After school, he would buy us pizzas and Twinkies. He always bought ice cream in unmarked transparent plastic buckets, wholesale, so we immediately knew the flavor by looking at the container. Before leaving the ice cream place, Papi would say, "Look, all American kids love this stuff." He watched television commercials to find out what American kids liked.

Once some boys from school took my brother André out of class and brought him to a candy store in a neighborhood he didn't know. They did this to all the Haitian kids at school who did not speak English. These boys told André they'd kill him if he didn't steal some candy and smuggle it out to them where they were waiting across the street from the store. After he took them the candy, André was deserted by the boys. He called the house crying and found my father there. When Papi brought him home, he said, "I thank God I drive a cab because I'm my own boss and I can be here day and night for you children."

Recently, after years of saving, my father and some friends started a car service business. Papi is the general manager. He still drives the Gypsy cab because the business is new and struggling, so he doesn't take a salary. Now he also works on Sunday afternoons when he used to watch Créole comedies and professional wrestling matches. My father does not like to accept money from my brothers and me. "It's very hard to be the guardian of other people's dreams. That can crush your own dreams." When he says this, it's hard to tell if he's talking about his past or about our future.

Now every Saturday my father gets up at 4:00 A.M. so he can pick up some passengers before the business opens at 6:00 A.M. My mother sits in the window watching him from their bedroom. She watches him as he turns on the ignition and combs what's left of his hair. The habitual nature of this morning ritual has rendered my father fearless. I am always frightened for him, since a man was found murdered in his car on our block a year ago. When the detectives came knocking on our front door in the middle of the night, my brother Kelly and I screamed "Papi!" until we remembered that he was asleep upstairs.

André always clips newspaper articles about Gypsy cab drivers murdered on the job and gives them to Papi, as a not-so-gentle warning for him to be careful, to be alert at all times. Sometimes André posts these clippings in my father's office at the car service so that the other drivers can see them too. My father often pulls them down and brings them home. He leaves the articles on his desk until one of us removes them.

A few years ago, a friend of my father's was murdered in his Gypsy cab, leaving behind a wife and four children. Some nights, when my father is late coming home, my brothers and I sit in the dark and talk, thinking about all the people we know about who have died that way. And always my youngest brother Karl says, "The angel of death has brushed Papi close quite a few times."

So now I always look with my mother as my father waits for his engine to warm up. He wraps his body around himself while blowing in his hands. As Papi sits there alone, I think of all the confidential chats he and I have had in the car, which has served as both taxicab and family car. "Talk to your brothers about how they're spending their money. They take a lot for granted. . . . Don't sit next to that man [an old beau] in church. Everyone will think you're back with him."

Now, with our grudge long settled, my father updates me on his insurance policy. He tells me what numbers to call and where the papers are kept. He tells me who owes him money. "In case I go suddenly, you collect." My mother and I are the only ones who are privy to that information. The boys might accidentally say something in passing and embarrass the borrower.

So now I watch as my father prepares to pull out into the cold morning, this Saturday at 4:00 A.M. The dark is menacing when someone you love is about to head out alone in it. His is the only car moving on the street, and soon it will turn away from our eyes.

My father is one of those people who can walk among others unnoticed. Yet he is to me, my mother, and my brothers a big chunk of life itself. When my father is with me, I can never keep my eyes off him. Something between wonder and worry makes me want to be near him so he can tap playfully on my shoulder, a nervous habit he has.

. . .

The filmmaker Jonathan Demme directed a short radio drama that I wrote to be broadcast on a station in Port-au-Prince. It was the story of a father who kills himself because he feels he is not living up to his own dreams or his family's expectations of him. Jonathan wanted my father to be in the radio drama. We knew that Papi would never agree to play the father role, which would require that he speak half the dialogue in the story. So we asked him to play a very small part as a factory foreman.

When the time came to record, I was terrified about having my father listen to the voices of the mother and the child in the story. They literally *loved* the father to death. Without realizing it, they drove him to extremes to please them and finally made him feel unworthy of their admiration. I most feared for my father hearing this line spoken by the actor playing the child: "I would rather die than be like my father whose life meant nothing."

Every time the actor spoke the line I saw my father wince. I knew his mannerisms well enough to read his expression. *Is that what she thinks of me?* I scolded myself, repeating the refrain of one of my closest friends, "Why can't you write happy things?"

On that day I wished I had written something happy, something closer to my father, truer to his own life. It's been said that most writers betray someone at some point in their lives. I felt that I had betrayed my father by not writing about a father who was more of a kindred spirit to him. Since I had the choice, I should have created a fighter, a survivor, a man who would never take the easy way out of life because he wanted to see "his children end up well."

In the studio that day, my father sat in a corner and prac-

ticed his few lines as the factory foreman. He even joked with
Jonathan about finally getting his chance to be the boss. When
his turn came, he recited the lines. He went over them a few
times before they had the right timbre.

Later, I wanted to explain. In the car on the way home, I
said, "Papi, you know it was a story."

He nodded. "Of course, of course. I understand."

I worried that I had wounded him, that somehow he'd feel
that everything he's done in his life has been for nothing. But a
few weeks later, I saw him put the tape of the radio play in his
car, before heading out in the night. He listened and he laughed
while waiting for his engine to warm up.

I remembered Jonathan saying, "You should have seen your
old man's face in the studio. He was beaming with pride." I
could not see it in the studio, but that day as my father sat in his
cab listening, I could see that he was seeing the obvious difference between that father and himself.

When I was a little girl, mad at my father for leaving me, I
used to have a recurring dream. I was running in a very dense
crowd looking for someone whose face I didn't know but whom
I expected to recognize on sight. The people in the crowd had
no faces except the one man at the very end, who was my father. Never have I seen my father's face so clearly as when I saw
it in that dream. Even in person, he's never been so alive yet so
serene, so beautiful.

Now, when I look at him over my mother's head through
their bedroom window on Saturday mornings at 4:00 A.M., I always have to remind myself not to compare my real father to
that dream. The man in that dream was not there. This father is.
And as my father is sitting in his car waiting for his engine to

warm up, I always wonder what is he thinking about? Is he thinking about the past, Beauséjour and Port-au-Prince, of that little girl who loved him so much that she was afraid to go near him for fear he might leave her again? Perhaps my father has now surrendered all that to the present, to the car, the engine, the cold, to the itch of balding, aging, and eczema.

I once asked Papi if he ever had any dreams about my brother André and me when we were still young in Haiti.

"Of course, of course," he said, "but there are too many to tell."

He did not just have the kind of dreams that you have while sleeping, he said. He had waking dreams; he saw our faces everywhere.

"And now every once in a while I see you in my waking dreams," I told him. "One day I would like to write about that."

"Yeah? If that is true, then will you do something for me?" he asked. "When you write about me give me some hair and decent skin. That will make me happy."

*Grandfather
Maximiliano
holding José Raúl*

Grandfather Maximiliano at dinner in 1956

JOSÉ RAÚL BERNARDO

In Cuba, where macho men strut by smoking huge thick cigars as visual metaphors for the sizes of their sexual members, cooking is an art form reserved exclusively for women, even in restaurants. And yet, as unbelievable as it may seem, cooking was something my grandfather, Maximiliano the butcher, dared to do. And he dared to do it well. Magnificently. However, before he would get into a kitchen, two conditions had to be rigorously met. The first was that since he was a butcher and he and his family ate meat day in day out, he would cook only seafood, shellfish being his great specialty. And the second was that he, being a man's man, would cook *only* for men, each of them being a close personal buddy of his, each of them having—like him—a large passionate appetite for everything important in a man's life: caiman hunting, deep-sea fishing, great sex, and, of course, great food.

To entertain this large bunch of hungry men, he would cook only at the large kitchen of El Club Cultural—pronounced El Kloob Kool-too-*ral*—a men's club located right by the ocean near La Habana, and only to celebrate an important event in the life of one of his buddies, who ranged from politicians to murderers, professions that in Cuba can easily be found in the one and same person. The menus he devised were aimed at satisfying the most demanding and at the same time the least delicate palates in the world. His cooking was certainly not for the weak. It reflected him: a corpulent man of Germanic ancestry with pale-blue eyes, golden bristly hair, and colossal strength, as tall and as handsome as the man he had been named after, the first and last emperor of Mexico, shot to death by the Mexican populace after introducing Viennese waltzes to mariachi bands.

I had not yet turned thirteen the first time I was invited to one of his feasts.

Well, I don't think "invited" is precisely the right word. He just told my father, "Bring José Raúl," and that was that.

The minute my father told me about the invitation I became so excited I began to count the days. I had never been to any of my grandfather's parties but I had heard a lot about them and I couldn't wait to meet all of those notorious *socios,* buddies of his, especially the honored guest at this party, a man who could have been my grandfather's twin, Papa Hemingway, and who had just finished the manuscript to a novel about a Cuban fisherman.

You can imagine my disappointment when the awaited Sunday finally arrived and I stepped, dressed in a suit and wearing the first long pants I ever owned, into the large central patio of El Kloob Kooltoo*ral,* just to find it completely empty of people. I thought that by the time we got there the room would be full of men, but my father and I had arrived early, bringing several huge netted bags filled with softshell blue crabs freshly caught by the two brothers Orihuela—crabs which my *abuelo* was planning to cook and serve at the banquet. I was left alone in the big empty patio while my father and the two brothers carried the crabs and a huge crate of avocados into the kitchen.

The two-story-high patio, lined with whitewashed walls, had been roofed for the occasion with white canvas stretched from one end of the space to the other, shading the patio from the brilliant tropical sun. Underneath this translucent canopy was a huge U-shaped table made up of many rectangular tables put together one against the other, covered with white linen tablecloths draping down to the floor, their fronts decorated with garlands of interwoven palm leaves.

I had just finished counting twenty-six place settings, neatly defined by starched white-linen napkins folded in the shape of pleated fans and inserted inside footed glasses—the kind I had seen only in the movies—when I saw my grandfather. He was coming down from his room upstairs, fresh from a shower, impeccably dressed in white—as always—and carrying in his right hand an electric fan, the kind that swivels. He saw me and, after tousling my hair—blond as his—he proceeded into the kitchen, removed first his jacket, then his shirt, hung them on a hook inside the huge kitchen, put on a white bib apron, plugged the fan in, turned it on, aimed it at himself, washed his hands thoroughly, and then shooed everybody out of his realm. No one but no one would ever know his cooking secrets. Absolutely no one.

Men began to arrive, and my father and the brothers Orihuela went to the entrance door, at the far end of the patio, to welcome them. I heard from afar my father's shouting and the hard slapping of shoulders as the men hugged tight and laughed loud, the way Cuban men greet each other.

Left on my own inside the large empty patio, I felt so thoroughly out of place that I didn't know what to do, so I began strolling around until, after a while, I found myself outside the kitchen, where one of the doors had been left ajar. My grandfather was inside, behind a huge pot of boiling water. By now he had taken off the bib apron, his pants, and his undershirt, and was wearing nothing but his baggy white-cotton drawers and the white shoes he always wore with white socks. He looked very funny, almost clownish, but I didn't dare to laugh. Nobody ever laughed at Maximiliano the butcher.

He noticed me looking at him and said "¡José Raúl!" as if I had just fallen from heaven. "Come here," he said. "We got to check all of these crabs, make sure they are male and alive." He saw the hesitation in my eyes. "It's easy. Here, let me show you how to grab them." I stepped inside. "But first," he added, "take off all of those clothes."

Before I realized it, all the female and the dead male crabs had been discarded; the rice had been measured, under his supervision, by me—now in my jockey shorts and shoes—and had been set aside next to a huge flat-lidded pot filled with the chicken stock he had prepared earlier that morning, to which he had just added a lot of saffron filaments that made the broth yellow; and now my *abuelo* was revealing to me what turned out to be the most important of his culinary secrets.

"Cooking is easy," he said, as he poured olive oil right from a large metal can into the saffron broth. "All you have to do is get the right ingredients, and put them together the right way."

He must have seen the baffled look on my face. "Think of ingredients as words, and of cooking as grammar. For a sentence to be clear we all have to follow the rules of grammar, don't we?" I assented by nodding my head. "Well," he added, "cooking is the same. You take a few words—ingredients—and you put them together the right way—grammar. As simple as that," he said. "And that is how most people cook," he continued as he stirred the hot broth. "The right ingredients put together the right way; what I call 'Cooking in Prose.' But"—he stopped his stirring and looked at me—"*some*times a sentence goes beyond just being clear. It becomes radiant. It illuminates your life. It may even change your life for good. And when that happens, *that* is poetry. *That* experience. *That* moment in your life." He looked at me as he smiled. "Have you ever felt it?"

I just looked up at him and said nothing. He must have sensed I didn't quite know what he was talking about.

"If you don't know what I mean, then you haven't experienced it yet. If you had, you would never be able to forget it, because, when it happens, time suddenly stops, just like that," he said as he snapped his fingers. "And when you come back to your senses, you feel as if you had just tasted a little bit of Paradise." He ladled a tiny bit of the hot broth into a tasting spoon. "Sometimes it even happens when you are cooking." He cooled the steaming broth in the spoon with his breath and tasted it. "Aahhh . . . ," he said, closing his eyes in ecstasy and nodding his head several times. "Now," he added, pointing to the stock, "*this* is what I call 'Cooking in Poetry.' "

He looked so funny in his old-fashioned white drawers and shoes sipping the broth while sweating and talking about poetry that I finally dared to chuckle.

"Don't laugh," he said, as he rinsed the tasting spoon in the sink. "Poetry can be found everywhere. Even in plain chicken broth. And when you find it, then you have to go 'Aahhh . . .' because no other word can describe that feeling." He looked at me, deep into my eyes, as he added, "So, when you cook— or when you do anything in your life—all you have to do is to strive for that Aahhh . . . , that magical moment when time stops. And once you experience it, once you find it anywhere in your life, then share it with the people you love." He went out the door leading from the kitchen into the service yard and brought in a case of beer he had placed there earlier to warm up in the hot sun. "Many years ago, when I was about your age," he said as he came in, "I discovered what poetry was for the first time in my life." He placed the wooden case filled with beer bottles on top of the tin-covered wood table he had been working on, making a loud clank. "And I found it in the strangest of places."

I looked up at him, and he immediately answered my unasked question.

"When I was cooking blue crabs, just like those." He pointed at the pile of live male crabs. Then, using a metal bottle opener screwed to the side of the worktable, he proceeded to open one bottle after another of that warm yeasty-smelling beer, pouring their contents into a huge deep pot until it was half full. "Now, hand me those crabs," he said.

I handed them to him, one at a time, grabbing them the right way, from behind, the way he had just taught me, to avoid being pinched by them.

"I didn't know it then," he added, "but I know it now, that blue crabs love sun-warmed beer. It makes them happy," he said as he delicately placed the crabs into the beer-laden pot, "and when they die, they die happy. And if one dies happy, one goes straight to heaven, so . . . well, I guess that's why they taste of heaven when you eat them. So there you are," he said as he looked at me and winked a smiling eye. "That's my cooking secret, which from now on is yours also."

I loved the complicity. I nodded, smiling back at him.

Once all the crabs were swimming in the warm beer, he threw the measured rice into the hot chicken-saffron stock, stirred it once, then covered it, and lowered the heat under it to almost nothing.

"And now," he said, "get dressed and go tell everybody that the meal will be ready in exactly twenty"—he looked at his watch and corrected himself—"nineteen minutes, and that I want you and the rest of the men in their chairs now. And I mean"—he loudly drummed the tin-covered worktable with the index finger of his right hand several times—"*Now!*"

I got dressed up again as fast as I could, though I had to do my tie three times and I still didn't get it the right length. Then, knowing that time was swiftly ticking away, I started to run across the patio to the bar at the other end, where the men were laughing loudly and every so often shouting *coño,* a Cuban four-letter word I was definitely not allowed to say at home, when, all of a sudden, a thought hit me so hard that it stopped me in my tracks: the sentence my grandfather had used. "You and the rest of the men," he had said. Which meant that in his eyes I was now one of them too. Me, *un hombre,* just like the rest of them. Me, one of Maximiliano's famous buddies!

Unaware of what I was doing I heard myself say "Aahhh . . ."

And then, after I heard myself say it—after I became aware of what had just happened—I felt different, very different, and

I wondered, Had I just experienced a moment of poetry? A moment when time had ceased to exist?

My grandfather had been right. It had felt good, really good, to experience a moment like that, when time suddenly stopped and I had a brief taste of paradise. And, as I realized that, I smiled at myself, and then ran across the patio to tell "the rest of the men" to come take their places at the huge U table "Now!" I sure didn't want to see my grandfather angry. Nobody ever wanted to see Maximiliano the butcher angry.

I sat at the huge U table, along with the rest of the men, and I laughed loud at their bad jokes, even at the ones I did not understand; and I even said one *coño* or two when the food was served, and I had not only seconds but thirds, and even a little bit of a fourth—something no other man, not even Papa Hemingway, known for his voracious appetite, did. When Maximiliano the butcher served it to me he said, "*Coño, hombre,* well done. Well done," and he heartily patted my back.

And though I had not swum in sun-warmed beer, I felt happy, very happy, as happy as one of those happy blue crabs, because I too had already tasted a little bit of paradise.

CALLIE

JAYNE ANNE PHILLIPS

There are two photographs of Callie, both in those dark sepia tones that look so brown and velvety. He was my mother's brother, and he died a year before she was born. My mother had a surviving brother and sister, but they were ten and twelve years older than she; to her, they seemed grown up from the beginning. Callie was the one who had disappeared, a baby she herself seemed to have lost, the child who would have changed her childhood. In one portrait he wears a smocked dress, stockings, buttoned shoes with straps, like any baby of that era. His moving hands are a blur. In the other he could be a contemporary two-year-old in a diaper, holding a ball; the haircut looks modern, and you can see faint lines on his calves where the stockings hugged his legs. He was a husky, healthy baby. Throughout her childhood, my mother heard his story in particular phrases. *He died of diphtheria and whooping cough. The girl brought it in with the butter.*

Callie

Before the Thornhill reversal of fortune, before they themselves kept cows and sold milk and butter, they had dairy goods
delivered by horse and wagon. The house in Belington was a
small Victorian mansion with stained-glass windows and warm,
burnished woods; there was a three-story floating staircase, but-
ler's pantry, buttons in the floor wired to sound in the long
kitchen at the back. Those fine old homes in isolated towns were
cut up into apartments later or turned into funeral homes. The
Thornhill home became a funeral parlor; it is a funeral parlor
today. Back then, in a West Virginia of 1924, the house was gracious, filled with the same antique furniture and dishes my family used as I was growing up, things my mother told stories
about. *Your grandmother rocked all her babies in this Eastlake cradle;
someday it will be yours.* I was my mother's only daughter, the one
who would inherit the dishes, the cradles, the women's things,
and the stories. *These are the Baltimore pear goblets that belonged to
your great-grandmother, here are the sugar, the creamer, the butter plate.*
The butter plate, round, of a glass so fine it rang, has a globular
lid, a round bell with the glass pear subtly swollen on the front.
They molded the butter to make it beautiful. When Mother used the
plate, I would ask for the story. She used to tell me, "Callie was my best
baby," and to the end of her life, her eyes filled with tears when she spoke
of him. Her best baby? I thought this an odd thing to repeat to a
surviving child, and told my mother so. *He never got to live,* my
mother retorted, exasperated. *What more could she give him, after
she'd lost him, but to say that? Good heavens, I didn't mind. It was a
terrible death for her.* Not the only death, but the worst one. *They
quarantined the house, and Mother fought it for four days and nights, the
fever and the terrible cough. Oh, you know the sound, like croup, like the
cry of a strange, barking bird, almost a nonhuman sound, and then they
stop coughing, and they drown.*

If you lose a child, the women of the town told me, it flattens you; you never get over it. But some women endured it repeatedly. I never knew my grandmother. But once I asked if she hadn't been angry at the woman who made the butter, the contaminated butter sold to those eight or nine houses, and her house was one. *How could she be angry? That woman didn't know, and she lost two children, her youngest baby and her older girl, too, the one who delivered the butter and helped her so. When Mother repeated that phrase she would weep, as though Callie had been her help. And he was. Until you came, she'd tell me.*

People don't always understand how babies can be a help, why seemingly beleaguered women might want another child, and another. If they can have them, if they can nurse them through what was once called childbed, and raise them. People forget, even women forget, how mothers fall in love with their babies. My grandmother's marriage was already a trial; her husband drank and philandered, and his business had begun to fail. The twin sons she'd lost a few years before were dead at birth; she never knew them. But she adored Callie. He looked like her own brother, Calvin, blond and fair as china, but his nature was his own. When she said he was her best, she meant that he was happy. One of those babies who is interested and alert but doesn't seem to resist the world, who seems delighted. He was peaceful, my mother was told, and his smile, the look of his eyes, lit up so. *The night he died he relaxed into Mother's arms and his little face turned resolute. His lips were blistered as though clear beads of water sat along his mouth. She'd tried so hard to save him.* The Belington graveyard was a rolling meadow, tamed and mown, fenced in Victorian black iron. Every spring they planted sweet peas and white impatiens at the smallest gravestones in the family plot. Two of the stones were sleeping lambs; one was a lamb that stood.

My mother learned vigilance from her mother. She wrapped her children up against the cold and never let them go out with their heads wet or too soon after a bath. She never let them sit on the ground, except at the height of summer; she said the ground was cold. She'd grown up alone with her mother, the other siblings having left home, the money gone. Her dissolute father was gone, committed to an asylum when she was sixteen, when the two women could no longer manage his moods and rages. They turned their big home into a rooming house and managed to keep the antiques, the silver, the dishes, the pewter. My mother taught me to value these things the family had touched and used; every holiday she set a festive, gracious table with the Haviland and the Baltimore pear.

I take the butter plate and its beautiful globe from my own shelves and think of my grandmother on a long-ago Easter, in another place and time. The girl has delivered the butter and my grandmother holds its pale color in her palms. She presses it into the mold by hand, flattening the top with a wooden spatula. When she turns it out onto the round butter plate it forms a flower shape nearly white, cool and creamy; the shape is round and compact as a girl's breast—a young girl, a girl the age of that twelve-year-old who just now finishes her rounds, having walked the last set of steps in her buttoned boots and collected the last of the money into her chambray clerk's apron. There is a dull throb in her head and her fingers tingle. It is April in the mountains and spring has just come. The air is crisp but the light has begun to change and the sky is breathy and blue. She woke even earlier than usual today, just after dawn, because her mother's babies were fussy and crying, because all the customers needed bigger orders than usual, in time for guests and Easter luncheons. Now the lurch of the wagon and the creaking of the big wheels begin to assert their dragging lull. She looks out into the road over the broad back of the harnessed mare and sees how the air seems to move and shimmer, as though it were a hot, hot day. She is warm and her face is moist. The ache in her head feels distant but more constant, a weight and a terrible pressure, as though a color of such density spreads through her. The horse knows the way, and so she closes her eyes.

ELIZABETH McCRACKEN

FAMILY

To see a well-regulated family acting as if they were one body informed by one soul, whose interests and hearts are inseparably united, acting in concert, adopting and making each other's cares their own, uniting their friendly beams, and jointly promoting the common happiness, is one of the most beautiful scenes.

—from *Goodykoontz's Perpetual Calendar and General Reference Manual—
A Book for the Millions,* by Jasper Goodykoontz (Atlanta, Indiana, 1900)

W as there ever such a family? My own has never behaved as one body informed by one soul, populated as it is by eccentrics, Midwestern visionaries, debaters, amateur comedians and philosophers, occasional lunatics. Genetically, we are strong on opinions. I can hear an assortment of relatives arguing, "One soul? Let me tell you why it should be mine."

Cousin Elizabeth

I received Jasper Goodykoontz's modest volume from my cousin Elizabeth, who, like the *Manual,* is a product of the turn-of-the-century Midwest: she was born two years before its publication, in Des Moines, where she still lives. The *Manual* is an old-fashioned compendium of wise and dumb advice, mathematical tables, form letters, and biographies of great men. Elizabeth is—well, this is the most important fact: she's a dancer. At ninety-seven, she still teaches ballet and tap. There is nothing old-fashioned about her.

Here's exactly how Elizabeth is related to me: she is my first cousin twice removed. Once upon a time (first in Russia, then on the east side of Des Moines), there was Elizabeth's Bubbe and Zayde, Samuel and Rifkah Jacobs. They had six children, whose names were, in descending order of age, Annie, Idy, Fannie, Mosey, Rosey, Hattie. Annie was Elizabeth's mother; Ida was my great-grandmother. My grandfather Harry Jacobson, Ida's only son, was Elizabeth's favorite cousin.

These people all live, quite clearly, in my head. I even know the ones I never met, largely because of photographs and the stories Elizabeth tells. I know that in one picture of all the Iowa first cousins, Irene (who died last year) is clutching peanuts in her fists, a bribe from the photographer to stop crying. I know that Aunt Rose, age five, circa 1884, is not grimacing but biting her lip, because Uncle Mose is reaching around to tickle her. I know that Zayde was a redhead and Uncle Mose was a wit. "Fannie," he once said, of a formal portrait of his older sister and a white terrier, "it's a *very* good picture of the dog."

To write about my cousin Elizabeth—my dearest cousin, the person I am named after—I need to tell you about her older sister Sarah, too, who lived with Elizabeth nearly all her life and played piano for dance lessons. I need to tell you about my mother's father, whom I never knew, and his wife, my grandmother, whom I most emphatically did. I need to tell you about the rest of the first cousins, at least the ones I've met, and their parents, and Bubbe and Zayde. I need to tell you about Elizabeth's children, my cousins Maisha and Frank, and Frank's sons, Rick and Ben.

Elizabeth is my family, which means no matter what I cannot separate her from everybody who leads to her, and how they lead to me. If she weren't a relative—if I were her neighbor, or student, or a reporter from a local paper—I could write an essay about a fascinating character: a Midwestern Jewish ballerina; a teacher with eighty years of experience who now gives lessons from a wheelchair; an artist who has always supported herself by her art; a successful small businesswoman; a mother who raised two children alone; a witty, occasionally acerbic conversationalist.

But I know Cousin Elizabeth, I love her, and all I can think about is what I'm leaving out.

DANCE

... To attempt to dance without a knowledge of the art is only to make yourself and partner ridiculous.

Goodykoontz's Manual

How to start? Perhaps a résumé. My family, especially my mother's side, has always been big on résumés and time lines, padded, when possible, with names of the famous (my grandmother once dated Louis Stuckey, heir to the Stuckey pecan roll fortune) and firsts (one of my antecedents was the first ordained Orthodox rabbi in Des Moines). I include these two examples because I know from reading nonfamily documents that the second is true, and I'm relatively sure my grandmother would not have made up the first. There are other celebrity connections and historical precedents that I'm less sure are purely factual, and am willing to pass along in bars but not in print.

I know Elizabeth's résumé fairly well, the important names: Albertieri, Ruth St. Denis, Miss Crawford, Rose Lorenz. Rose Lorenz was Elizabeth's chief rival in the Des Moines dance studio business, and taught the Leachman girls, including young Chloris. Says Elizabeth, "Rose Lorenz wanted to have the biggest studio in Des Moines, and I wanted to have the best, and we both succeeded."

These days, Des Moines gets a *Star Search* champion in the road show of *Joseph and the Technicolor Dreamcoat,* while the big cities get Donny Osmond. As children in Des Moines, at the height of vaudeville, Sarah and Elizabeth, the Werblowsky sisters, saw Eubie Blake, a young Josephine Baker ("I still remember her exit," says Elizabeth, "cakewalk kicks, which were wa-a-ay up there, all the way off") and Bill "Bojangles" Robinson, whom they went to see because he was billed as The Chocolate Nijinsky.

When Elizabeth was fifteen, she accompanied Sarah to Miss Crawford's dance studio, where Sarah, age twenty-two, attended "The Business Girls Class." In other words, a class for girls without husbands, girls for whom dance lessons were an investment in possible future happiness. The students learned to dance by dancing with each other. At the end of the lesson, Miss Crawford chose Elizabeth as her partner.

That's how it started. Elizabeth's mother, recently widowed, did not approve. Sister Sarah made it clear: if Elizabeth wanted to dance, she'd have to earn the money to do it. How could she earn money before she started? "That's a good question," she says. "It shows how much other people knew about dance."

Elizabeth graduated from high school. Miss Crawford found her jobs: first in Mason City, Iowa, then assisting in the studio. One summer, the two of them went to California to study with Ruth St. Denis and Ted Shawn. A fellow student told her she was a natural for modern dance.

"Well, you know me," Elizabeth says. "I didn't want to do it. If I'm a natural, why study it?"

Back in Des Moines, she taught classes when Miss Crawford wasn't there. "I was teaching all those dances she had supposedly learned. She had notebooks full of them. I didn't have notebooks: I had my head full." Every Saturday, Elizabeth gave lessons at Miss Crawford's from nine until six. Sarah told her to ask for a raise.

"I was making fifteen dollars a week, so I wanted twenty-five—and she said, 'E-*liz*-a-beth. You're asking me to split my business with you.' And I said, nevertheless, I want a ten-dollar raise. She insisted no, and so I left her. I put a little one-column ad in the paper, and that's all I did. My name, *Dance Studio,* and a telephone number. And in the first week, I had all my classes lined up."

That was in 1918. After a year she had saved enough money to go to New York with her mother and sister. While looking for an apartment, she ran into Irene Marmein, half of a vaudeville act, who suggested that Elizabeth study with Luigi Albertieri, formerly the principal dancer with the Metropolitan, now giving private lessons.

"Lucky, very lucky," says Elizabeth. "I told him I wanted to study with him that day. And he said he had a class at twelve. I said, No, no, no, this is an advanced class, I'll come back at four for the beginners. And he said, No, no, no, you stay right here and take the lesson. And of course, I fell down doing some sort of combination, as I remember it. The most terribly hard thing in the world, and I fell to the floor. And he walked out. The class hung around in the studio off the barres, giving me daggered looks, acting like I was the biggest impostor they'd ever seen, and what was I doing there, and would I get out of their sight. And Albertieri picks up his cigar—a cheroot, he used to smoke—and walks back in and on the way in hits me with his cane, which I later found out was a sign of deep affection. And he pointed to the corner: I should try again. And when I said to him at the end of the class, Maestro, I need to come back at four, this isn't the place for me, he said, No, no, no—what you don't know today you'll learn tomorrow."

And she did. "He knew everything, and I knew nothing, and together we were a pair. He didn't teach at all, if you know what I mean. You had to absorb it like a sponge. But I was a sponge."

She came back to Des Moines with what she knew. In 1931, she spent six months in Chicago—"I heard that Nobikoff was there, and thought I'd like to dance with him." Nobikoff had been a partner of Anna Pavlova; while taking his class, Elizabeth was asked to join the Chicago Opera Ballet. She was over thirty—"over the barre," she calls it. "But you can't stop some people."

All this time, Sarah had been paying rent on Elizabeth's studio, waiting for her to come back to Des Moines. When the company went on the road, Elizabeth went home.

She taught ballet, she taught tap, she taught social dancing. For Iowa's centennial, she organized one hundred dancers for a performance at the state fair. "Didn't cost the state a cent. A hundred people all en pointe. Well, everyone except maybe three or four. But I needed them, because I wanted one hundred people."

She was—and is—an exacting teacher. "If you want to come in just to learn a step, and not the subject, you're foolish to study with me. You don't have to study with me to learn two flaps and three shuffles. That's not the point. You have to learn the subject."

My love for Elizabeth has been handed down from the generations. My mother was born with orthopedic difficulties, and spent her childhood in casts and hospital rooms, in waiting rooms and on train rides to the next specialist. Her childhood home housed, in its basement, a giant metal tank for her water exercises. Nevertheless, no doctor could come up with a cure for her chronically sore neck; it was Elizabeth who devised the exercise that strengthened her muscles. In six weeks, the problem disappeared. Mom worked with Elizabeth every day for much of her childhood—not so much lessons as dealing with specific problems and coming up with a system to solve them. "Your system will be different from someone else's," Elizabeth said. It was Elizabeth my mother went to when, in high school, she could not quite figure out how to walk down the halls carrying heavy textbooks. Elizabeth calls the day my mother walked down the aisle to deliver her high school valedictory address one of the unforgettable moments of her life.

And it was Elizabeth who taught my mother how to do somersaults. This was something the doctors no doubt never would have predicted—would probably have advised against—

but my mother remembers the party where, under Elizabeth's direction, they showed off their mutual triumph.

When I remind Elizabeth, she says, "Backward *and* forward, Sphinx, never forget that. She did both."

Elizabeth can turn anything into a dance. On my last visit, she was, after breakfast, quietly belching.

"I have Vesuvius within," she said. I offered to throw her over my shoulder and pat her back like a baby's.

"Oh," she said, "I think that's delightful. Adagio for burps."

NAME, GOOD

. . . A name, whether good or bad, true or false, may be compared to the face by which one is known. It is the most valuable garment by which one is wrapped, and soon as is spoken or seen, creates favor or prejudice.

Goodykoontz's Manual

My mother always knew she'd name a daughter for her favorite cousin. I once mentioned this to my grandmother, who was adamant that my mother would never have done anything so out-of-step with Jewish tradition as to name a child after a living relative. (This shock from a woman, a serious and devout Reform Jew, who nevertheless always secularly and unembarrassedly celebrated Christmas and Easter, since they were such good excuses for gift-giving and eating, and besides the family dimestore stocked decorations. She probably would have celebrated Ramadan, had it fulfilled these requirements.)

"You were named after your father's sister," Grandmother told me, and would not discuss it further. Nothing scandalous about being named after *that* side of the family.

Now Elizabeth calls me Sphinx, because of my tendency to sit cross-legged on the floor. I love the name; it has a pleasant, jazz-age sound to it, and I can always pretend it has to do with my mystery instead of my posture.

"Sphinx," she says before she starts a story, "listen carefully, dear." Or: "Mama was an extraordinary person, Sphinx, I didn't realize it then." She has that knack for saying your name to you often enough that it starts to sound like praise: she wants you to know she wouldn't spend her time telling this to just anyone.

Name-changing is a tradition. Elizabeth's given name is Libby, but Sarah thought, once Elizabeth reached high school, that she needed something more sophisticated. My grandfather's family always referred to the Werblowskys as The Ws, pronounced the Midwestern way: *Let's go to visit the Double-yas.* Sixty-five years after her marriage, Elizabeth is listed under both Werblowsky and Perowsky in the phone book. I once heard her inform some very confused door-to-door solicitors that she didn't prefer one over the other. But which one do you use? they asked. Either, said Elizabeth, it really doesn't matter to me.

HOME

The personality of the mistress of the house, pervades its atmosphere. . . .

A house may have the appearance of refinement without any great expense, if good taste be exercised in its arrangement. Furnish the rooms with an artistic eye for colors, and a careful eye for comfort.

Goodykoontz's Manual

As a child, I loved Elizabeth's house. There were trunks full of costumes, lace fans, dolls dancing in Spanish dresses. There were photographs from the thirties with fond inscriptions, some in foreign languages; there was even—and this was something I thought particularly spectacular—a painting of Elizabeth. I'd never known someone who owned a painting of herself.

Not that she likes it. She says, of the friend who painted it, "You'll notice she gave it to me. *She* didn't want it around."

The front door of the house opens right into the dance studio, a long room with a fireplace at the end. The wood floor is pale and dull, polished by the suede bottoms of hundreds of ballet shoes shushing across, in some places dimpled by taps. The barres have been oiled by sixty years' worth of hands, and the mirror on the far wall is chipped, nearly ghostly. I love to sit on the steps that lead from upstairs into the studio, and watch a lesson: two women, for instance, taking tap, Frank Sinatra singing, "They Can't Take That Away from Me," Elizabeth parked near the doorway, conducting with her hand. Sometimes she sings along. She enunciates, *dee-dah-dee-dah-dee-dah*.

The grand piano in the corner belonged to Sarah, who died eight years ago, at the age of ninety-six. Since its mistress's demise, the piano's used mostly as a giant end table, topped by sheet music, cassette tapes, CDs, a pair of felt hats still used in student tap routines. It's hard to see a piano without trying out a key or two, but now the only answer is a mournful abandoned untuned *plunk*.

The sitting room beyond the studio has dark oriental wallpaper patterned with birds and bamboo trees; the wood trim is scarlet. A plate rail running around the room holds recent and forever treasures: a cranberry glass cup with her name on it (a souvenir from Aunt Rose's visit to the 1904 World's Fair); a straw hat used as a prop in a dance; a Chinese drum bought in New York upon her grandson Benny's birth (he turned out to be a drummer); a sampler stitched by her mother on the boat from Russia, postdated one year, 1882, because twelve-year-old Annie thought sailing to America surely would take at least a year. There is Elizabeth's small beer bottle collection, which she took up two years ago and stopped when the plate rail got full. (She did not empty the bottles herself—she does not drink, and has never tasted beer.)

She moved into the house in 1932, and little inside has changed: the same punch light switches (upper button on, lower off), the same porcelain bathroom fixtures, the same dark furniture. The walls have been repainted their 1930s colors: pale green, deep red. Of course, dance paraphernalia is everywhere: shoes, dolls, snowglobes with ballerinas at their heart, posters, photographs. Here's a picture of Elizabeth and eight young women balanced en pointe; here's a pencil drawing by a young artist who, years ago, dropped by to sit on the stairs and watch lessons. A photo of Albertieri hangs by the door, a plump round-headed handsome man dressed in a peasant costume. The only words in the Italian inscription I can make sense of: *bravissima, etudia, Elizabetta.*

FACE

A face which is always serene possesses a mysterious and powerful attraction. Faces are more legible than books, and may be read at a glance.

Goodykoontz's Manual

It's impossible and irresistible to imagine what those we love were like in the long years before we met them. In Elizabeth's case, I have some help: a profusion of photographs, formal, candid, theatrical. Elizabeth's hair is now as snow white as it used to be coal black; she wears it combed forward. Her nose is long— aristocratic, I'd say—and her eyes are dark behind her glasses. Her moderate smile uses every muscle in her face, except the ones that actually operate her mouth; the more extravagant version is a silent, delighted laugh. I have always thought her extraordinarily beautiful.

Recently we looked through a snapshot album from Elizabeth's youth. Most of the pictures were taken in 1915, full of pretty girls in middy blouses posing with great formal silliness, one leg turned out, a hand on a hip. Elizabeth had written captions for quite a few of them, silvery pencil on black paper; I had to tilt the album to read the words. One picture showed her older sister, Sarah, kneeling on a lawn and laughing, combing her long hair with her fingers. Underneath it, Elizabeth had written, *Siren*. That picture shocked me more than any photo of Elizabeth ever could. I remember Sarah as one of the most reserved people I've ever known. I never knew she had long hair, never imagined her laughing other than wryly, never pictured her nearly that beautiful. In 1915, Sarah was twenty-four. She had, Elizabeth says, a dry wit. She never married. The family lore says that she had her heart broken.

(Which is the family lore about any woman who never married. I always wonder whether it's true, or whether as a woman grew older, alone, past marrying age—by which I mean sixty, there is a family history of late marriages—it seemed too sad to acknowledge that she'd never even passingly known romantic love, ignoring all the perfectly good varieties of love and career she *was* expert at. Better to think she'd tasted romance and thereafter turned it down, a bad piece of fish, liver and onions. I hate to admit I'd rather think so, too, even though I realize it's something my future nieces and nephews may one day be told about me.)

But Elizabeth is always Elizabeth in pictures: a black-eyed baby; a poised six-year-old; dancing with a garland of flowers in front of a flat backdrop; in her backyard, folding her hair to her nape to display an impossibly long neck; brandishing a small cigar (a prop for a dance that also involved a turban and a parasol); leaning on her car in the 1950s, on her way to New York with her son and daughter. So beautiful in every picture, white-skinned and black-haired, narrow-hipped, small-mouthed. And always Cousin Elizabeth, always herself, though I never saw that glossy black hair, though she quit driving years ago.

SORROW

. . . Sorrow is not without its uses. We darken the cage of a bird to make it sing; night brings out the stars; and sorrows reveal to us many truths.

Goodykoontz's Manual

She married Frank Perowsky in 1931. They'd met at a dance at the Jewish Community Center, and he walked her home. (He'd driven there, but figured she'd turn down a ride.) Ten months after the wedding, they had their daughter, Maisha. They moved together to the house on Forty-fourth Street. Then, when Elizabeth was three months pregnant with their second child, Frank went into the hospital for an appendectomy. He died there of an aneurism, by coincidence or neglect. She named their son Frank; he turned out to be a fragile kid, hospitalized for digestive problems off and on until he was five years old. Now he's sixty-one, a professional saxophonist in New York City, where he's lived since he was eighteen and Elizabeth drove him across country to attend Juilliard. Elizabeth still calls him Frankie.

Maisha is mildly retarded, though when I was a child I thought she was simply a few years older than I was. I don't know exactly how I could have thought this, except that I was always short for my age and other kids seemed very (although never threateningly) large. I don't know what I made of her already graying hair. I still remember the walk with Maisha when I realized my mistake, though not what tipped me off. Maybe I'm wrong and never formulated so complex a theory concerning her age; maybe it was just during that walk that I realized that she was definitely a different sort of grown-up who happened to be a little older than my mother: I was never told that Maish was retarded. She was—and is—simply Maisha, funny and good-hearted and possessor of complex and reliable memory.

Elizabeth never remarried. "I had my hands full," she says. At the age of thirty-six, she was suddenly a single mother. Sarah moved in, played piano for lessons, helped out.

And yet Elizabeth is not even vaguely a tragic figure, a sorrowful person. Anytime I have ever heard someone suggest to her that she must be very brave to have survived all she has, she makes a face, says, No. Her point is not that her life did not have its extraordinarily sad moments, but that there was nothing to do but survive them. Whatever small alternatives there are—dying, nervous breakdowns, self-pity, or self-congratulations—are unpalatable.

About tragedy she is practical. The person she feels sorriest for is the person who lost the most: Frank Perowsky, her young husband, the once and future father. "Think of all he's missed, by not being here," she says. "Think of how he would have loved Frankie." She pauses. "The *fun* they would have had together."

She was married for two and a half years. She has been widowed for more than sixty.

And still: "I reach out for him, and he isn't there, and he isn't there. He should be there, Sphinxy."

Yes.

"It's a story without end. It's all ends, that's all it is, but it's without end."

I never knew Elizabeth before she was widowed, when Maisha was little and the three of them moved into the brick house on Forty-fourth Street with the huge living room (not yet a dance studio) and all those bedrooms upstairs. I don't know what she was like when Frankie went into the pediatric wing of Mercy Hospital, his skin burnt up from the disinfectant they washed the sheets with. I don't know exactly how her life has changed her, though I know it has. One of the things we have in common—besides a fondness for Gene Kelly and a tendency to collect souvenirs of all sorts—is an abiding interest in the deeper character of people. She's sentimental about everyone she loves, whether they are living or dead, celebrities or across-the-street neighbors. When Elizabeth thinks highly of someone, she says, "She is not a usual person" or "He may look ordinary, but he's not." She is especially admiring of people who have overcome tragedies; I don't know whether this is because of her own.

We talk about her students, her friends, people in the news. She sends me clippings from the Des Moines *Register:* a woman who tried to drown her baby; another who died at the age of ninety-two and who made Thanksgiving dinner annually for her many descendants, basting the turkeys in white wine. On the point of one envelope, Elizabeth wrote, in her spidery handwriting, *stimulus?*

"What people have to bear in this world, Sphinx," she says. She has said it to me more than once, though never in reference to herself.

Her tombstone, Elizabeth says, will be Shalom Home, a residence for mentally retarded adults, which she co-founded so that Maisha would have a place to live forever. She doesn't mean tombstone literally, of course; she plans to be cremated, as Sarah was (and whose tombstone is currently the front hall closet door, since that's where her ashes are).

Shalom Home is a Jewish home, though not all the people who live there are Jewish. "We're allowed to stay at the Catholic hospital," says Elizabeth, "and I know I don't get offended at the crosses in the rooms. We need to make our contribution to the community." As far as she knows, it's the first such home in the country—"followed almost immediately by one in Minneapolis." Judaism is, of course, not unheard of in Des Moines, but neither is it common, and Shalom means that Maisha and the other Jewish residents will always have a *Jewish* home, a place where their traditions are understood and available, unexotic, unexceptional.

FOOD

Avoid abuse and excess, as there is sure to follow a period of suffering in mind and body, either in sickness, ill temper, or vicious inclinations, or all of them at once.

Goodykoontz's Manual

"I would not dream of eating an olive," Elizabeth says and, in fact, never has. Olives are the least of it: she does not eat vinegar or oil, avoids onions, despises sauces and gravies of any kind. Salad dressings are especially offensive. She's fond of attributing her long life to abstention from certain foods, which I can believe when she credits an aversion to oil but am skeptical of when it comes to garlic. To which she always says, "But can you argue?" and, of course, I can't. For a long time, the only beverage she took was coffee, though recently she's acquired a root beer habit.

This is Elizabeth's diet: ice cream, coffee, hard candy, brisket, french fries, pizza, chocolate, buttered toast, iceberg lettuce, peanut butter, and a cashew chicken dish served in a pineapple available from a Thai restaurant downtown. The peanut butter is the important menu item. Every morning she has, for breakfast, toast with butter and peanut butter. The butter is in a cut-glass dish, kept on the counter; the peanut butter is chunky style.

For a while the counter nearly always featured a banana that had been sliced in half through the skin, the cut end sealed with a piece of plastic wrap secured by a rubber band. She hates bananas, but a doctor told her she needed the potassium. Recently she decided there was no point in eating anything she didn't like. She also once told me, "The only medication I take is Centrum."

In grad school I wrote a story for a class in which a ninety-year-old woman ate a brisket sandwich. I hadn't thought this unusual. The teacher objected: it was unrealistic, no ninety-year-old ate brisket. Okay, I said, if I wanted to write a convincing story in which there was a ninety-year-old who ate brisket, how would I go about it? Impossible, he said, no such animal.

So I have had to wait until I wrote a piece of nonfiction to report these facts: Elizabeth has her own teeth, and her brisket is very tender.

FRIENDSHIP

> On the broad highway of action,
> Friends of worth are far and few;
> But when one has proved her friendship,
> Cling to one who clings to you.

Elizabeth was good friends with my grandmother, her darling cousin Harry's widow. When my grandmother died, two years ago at the age of ninety, the person I worried most about was Elizabeth. The two of them were wonderful together. They both had careers as small businesswomen long before most women did—Elizabeth with her studio, Grandmother with her husband's store—and both were Midwestern Reform Jews with an interest in the daily application and tradition of their religion. Both served as president of the board of Shalom Home. Very different, too. Grandmother was extremely stylish, with dyed blond hair ("That's your grandfather's first wife," she'd say, pointing to pictures of herself as a brunette), tailored clothing, and manicured nails. Elizabeth, on the other hand, has always dressed like an artist, her hair loose, her clothes comfortable and vividly colored, costume jewelry. Their deepest natures reflect this: my grandmother accomplished a great deal fueled by worried energy; Elizabeth has accomplished a great deal fueled by a belief that there is no reason not to accomplish a great deal. She would also be the first person to point out that her sister, a pessimist, was willing to do the worrying for both of them.

Grandmother once told me a story about one of their early meetings. Before she married Harry Jacobson, Grandmother knew Elizabeth was important to him; his letters during their short courtship are full of references to the Double-ya household. So my grandmother, the new bride (another woman who might be expected not to marry, since she was nearly thirty and definitely a career girl), invited Elizabeth and Sarah over to dinner. She prepared, she told me, "an elaborate feast." It was winter.

Elizabeth showed up early because she wanted to go sledding, and so she did, and came into the dining room, and doffed her snowy pants (pants!) and sat down to dinner in her leotards. Which, of course, she was quite used to wearing in public.

My grandmother told this with the sort of fondness that could only have been born out of initial horror. She told it as much on herself as on Elizabeth; now that they were friends, she couldn't imagine why she had thought it so peculiar; and she also couldn't quite imagine—still—that it was a good idea to come to a dinner party in a leotard and tights.

CONVERSATION

Always appear pleased, though it is an oft told story, and the speaker an inveterate proser; in short, sacrifice sincerity as good manners and feelings dictate. . . .

To skilfully adapt one's conversation to the hearers, is the secret of speaking well.

Goodykoontz's Manual

Once, when I said of a person who annoyed us both, "Well, God bless her," Elizabeth said, "Well, if He has any spare time, sure. Otherwise, He shouldn't bother."

To say that Elizabeth is certain of her opinions is one of the understatements of the twentieth century. She is not rude, not at all, but there is not much sincerity sacrificed in her conversation.

At a Ballet Iowa performance, we ran into a man whom she'd known—and, it turned out, disliked—as a boy. He instantly annoyed me by saying, "I wonder if she remembers me?"

"I remember you, Joe," said Elizabeth.

He let us in on a secret: because there was never a good audience at the ballet in Des Moines, you could just buy a cheap ticket, and then move down to a better seat.

"No reason not to, right?" he said.

"Not unless you think the ballet is a good cause and you want to support it," said Elizabeth.

I tell people about Cousin Elizabeth, generally in answer to the question, *Why on earth are you going to Des Moines?* They say, *Does she live at home?* And *Is she, you know, all there?*

Because, of course, most people her age don't, aren't. Elizabeth recently went to a birthday party at what was once called The Jewish Home for the Aged and is now The Iowa Jewish Senior Life Center. ("Life?" says Elizabeth. "Anything but.") One of her husband's cousins, an old dear friend, was turning one hundred. Only her body was in attendance.

"Oy, oy, oy," says Elizabeth. "It was a sad little group."

When we go out together in Des Moines, we nearly always meet someone who knows her—students, people she directed in community theater. If they haven't seen her for a while— and if they are dumb—they lean in and speak to her slowly, sort of mentally grinding food. She's an old lady, after all; important not to give her something too strenuous to mull over. *Good Lord,* you can hear them think, *she must be nearly a hundred by now.*

It's rather delicious when Elizabeth answers them, sometimes impatiently, "Yes, dear. What have you been doing since *Guys and Dolls?*"

Her hands are arthritic, but still useful, and still graceful. When she studied with Albertieri, someone complained that Elizabeth was dancing with the advanced students: clearly she belonged in the beginners' class. "Look at the arms," said Albertieri, "they're what make a dancer." Her legs, Elizabeth says now, were useless. She once explained to me one of Albertieri's theories of dance, which she agreed with: the legs are technique, and the arms are emotion. (It was one of many times we have had conversations about how dance is like writing, how emotion and technique are inextricably connected, but somehow separate.) Her arms are still the emotion: they gesture, point at abstract ideas, indicate indifference and passion and irony. Her legs are now really useless, the cumulative effects of a hip replacement, then a broken hip, then, a year and a half ago, a broken femur.

She quit dancing, she says, long after she should have, long after most people do, demonstrating to her students until her seventies. Still, it's been twenty-five years.

"Sometimes I think I made it up, Sphinx. Except I've got a few pictures."

I have never seen her dance.

INDIVIDUALITY

Individuality of constitution we have by nature, and individuality of character we may have by achievement. Everyone has, by nature, special instruments by which to make himself, and achieve his mission, but alas! how few there are who do not use borrowed instruments. The greatness of any one depends primarily on what he has peculiar to himself.

Goodykoontz's Manual

Elizabeth is a Robert Browning fan and has many of his poems memorized; she puts herself to sleep by mentally reciting "Rabbi Ben Ezra," which begins, "Grow old along with me! The best is yet to be." She has worn the same pin, a mask made by a dancer friend—a fellow student from Albertieri's class—every day since it was given to her in the early 1930s. Her collection of paper ephemera makes my own only the second largest in the family: restaurant place mats signed by her dining companions, envelopes with articles of interest, magazines, sheet music, temple bulletins. Her downstairs bathroom is entirely papered with advertisements for and reviews of Frank and Benny's performances.

Common wisdom—so often wrong and wrongheaded—says that as people age, they do not change except to become more like themselves. But I've never known anyone who has lived past the age of seventy-five—and I've known a lot of them—who did not become more fond, more open, more sentimental in the best sense of the word. Maybe age means becoming more flexible; maybe only flexible people survive. Time goes on, and you deepen, you change your habits, you finally say something that you've meant to for a long time. You learn to say good-bye better, you learn to complain when riled.

But Elizabeth remains the one person I know over the age of seventy who consistently picks up new quotidian habits. The beer bottle collection, for instance, and a fondness for long ethnic earrings—this she acquired six years ago when her head was shaved for brain surgery. If you're wondering what a ninety-year-old woman looks like with a buzz cut, well, she looked great. My grandmother tried to talk her into wearing a wig. Not bloody likely.

Three years ago she began writing poetry and has amassed enough that her grandson Ben collected it into a handmade book. One of her poems is about her fondness of traveling on wheels, from roller skates to cars to her wheelchair. In fact, for someone so used to taking care of herself, she's adjusted well to needing assistance. Now that she finally has live-in help, she's taken to calling herself the Queen of Sheba.

Though she certainly isn't idle. She says, "I was talking to Maisha. Most people have two sides to their life. I think I had three chances. Three distinct parts of me. I had this quiet Midwest home, which you know I loved, been here since I was back from the Opera. If I'd stayed with the Opera company, see, I wouldn't have had that. I had my studio. Third career, dear, is braille." For sixty years, Elizabeth has brailled for the Iowa Commission for the Blind, first on a manual machine, now on a computer that is slightly nicer than mine. Every day, she does a page.

Her latest project is my collection of short stories; and when I talk to her she reports her progress. Though she understands, with a clarity that many of my relatives do not possess, that what I write is fiction, made up, and not about me or my family, she slipped up once. A character refers to herself as a knock-kneed dancer.

"I came to that part of the book where you say you can't dance," she said. "Sphinx, I don't like that you think you can't dance."

Well, I can't dance, it's true. That part *was* autobiographical.

Maybe I should try. It's the worst thing Elizabeth can think of: a person who won't dance because she thinks she can't.

She is writing my book over, in a new language. It makes me want to cry. She told me it's her last brailling project, and maybe it is. She said, "How long can one person live? Not forever! Not forever." Then she said, "I don't mind living, dear, you know that. What I don't want to happen is to hang around. That I don't want and you don't want it for me either. So as long as I'm me, I'm delighted to be here. I still have work to do, I think."

Well, maybe forever. Forever would be nice.

The thing is, we're soul mates. We have the best conversations. Despite our nearly seventy-year-age difference, I don't think of her as my elder. Odd, I know, but somehow the important part of our relationship is *cousin* and not *twice removed*. There's a certain carelessness of expectation that skips generations, what children expect of their parents, what parents expect of children. We're just always delighted to see each other.

We talk about our favorite subjects, Art and People. We can talk about family forever, supplying each other with facts the other never knew, wondering what got into the head of this aunt, what exactly Bubbe thought, what might have happened to Uncle Mose, the wit, if he'd been born into another family and had been encouraged to be a comedian instead of a shop owner. There are six generations we can talk about now, from Bubbe and Zayde to her grandson Rick's son, Joel.

I have said Elizabeth is my family. She has given me my family, too, in her stories. She has given me my schoolgirl mother down on the exercise mat, pulling her knees to her chin, to her nose, to her forehead, till all of a sudden she's on the other side sitting up, how about that. She has given me my grandmother, the Independent Thinker, as a new bride in Valley Junction, Iowa—and it's almost as if it's me she isn't related to yet, my family she's marrying into, but look out, here she comes, soon we'll all love her. She has given me my grandfather, Harry Jacobson— my brother's namesake; we're Harry and Elizabeth, too—as a kid miserable in a battenburg lace collar tatted by his mother; as Bubbe's absolute favorite and nobody minded; as a young businessman leaving his store for an emergency: Elizabeth cooked him some beans and they were getting cold. She has given me Annie, Idy, Fannie, Mosey, Rosey, Hattie, the Jacobs kids: Annie who ran the house because Bubbe was always pregnant; Ida, my grandmother, who married M. L. Jacobson, M. L. who was such a darling; Fannie, the flawless seamstress; Mose, the tragic wit; Rose, who married a man named Quigley and moved to California; Hattie, who married Mr. Skirble, awarded by the family the honorific because, unlike Quigley, he was Jewish. Because of Elizabeth, I know what's happening in a photograph taken one hundred ten years ago. Because of Elizabeth, I know that my great-great-grandfather was a redhead, and so cute. Zayde was always so cute.

And I have Elizabeth, too, walking down the street in New York City sometime before 1920. Tomorrow she'll meet Albertieri, but she doesn't know that yet, she just knows that she's come to New York to dance, that this is the place to do it, that dancing is all she wants in life. It's before she's fallen in love; before Frank, before Maisha, before Frankie; before most of the people I know have stepped into her life. Sarah and Mama are at the hotel. Maybe they're asleep. Maybe everyone in New York is asleep. She is a beautiful Midwestern girl a thousand miles from home who up and left, and made no definite plans, but here she is. She is willing to learn. She is willing to listen.

WHITNEY OTTO

1980

John impulsively rescues Kali from the San Francisco Animal Shelter, where, after an extended stay, she is due to be put to sleep. He brings her home to the large Mission District Victorian that he shares with two female roommates who work such weird, nocturnal hours (at a Bank of America no less) it is as if he lives alone.

My residence is a modern condominium in Marin County. I also live with two women, only my situation is a little less congenial, which is a shame because we all used to like one another. And I love San Francisco (a place that makes my roommates nervous), and I don't much like Marin, and my job is awful.

When I first see Kali she is perched on the edge of John's bed, in his perpetually dark room, with its single, elongated

Kali and J.B.

window that looks out on another single, elongated window. I find her rather unattractive and greasy-looking. I ask, John, what possessed you?

He explains how popular she was at the pound, and how wonderfully casual she was when he stopped at her cage, as if she were looking him over. I think she has potential, he says.

We name her Kali Mountain after a hillside in Jamaica, where, we are told, ganja grows. But she is mostly called Kali. This is in April.

In June, John's brother stops briefly in the City on his way to work in a cannery in Seward, Alaska. He is following a girl (also set to work in the cannery for the summer) that he fell in love with the previous month. John decides to join him. I cry a good deal over the next two days because I'll miss John and I don't want to be left behind in Marin, with a job I hate and roommates who I think are mildly sadistic. He says, I'll be back before you know it. He asks me to come with him, but I'm not the carelessly-abandon-everything-in-two-days kind of girl, and I remind him that I have a job and two roommates to consider.

He can't understand why I would forgo adventure to remain in an unhappy situation, and, frankly, neither can I, but there you are. I remind him that unlike the three of them (John, his brother, and his brother's girl), I am no longer in college. However, there is more to my reticence than that: we get handed all kinds of genes at birth and mine is the responsibility gene. I am not proud of this trait. I would love nothing more than to live a life of reckless abandon. Unfortunately, the responsibility gene did not come in tandem with the neatness gene, giving me the worst of all worlds: a messy house I cannot leave.

John's departure means I inherit Kali. My roommates are not happy about this, but then none of us are very happy with one another in general. Kali becomes my only friend in the house, and once uses my roommate's bed as a cat box, creating a fairly vile mess, and even as I am apologizing and cleaning it up, I am secretly thanking Kali for treating my roommate the way I feel she has been treating me for the past four months.

John returns from Alaska and the three of us—Kali, John, and myself—move to a small, crummy studio in San Francisco. John and I have been together two years.

1981

Living together is not like sleeping over at each other's house a few times a week. It is more like living together, which, I imagine, is rather like marriage. John and I are sure we love each other but we are uncertain about sharing an address.

We adopt a German shepherd–mix puppy and an almost unpleasantly strange white Manx kitten. Both are from the pound, Kali's previous home. She hates these interlopers and makes her feelings known by glowering from the top of the refrigerator for three days.

1982

We finally move out of our dreadful, crowded studio. We say good-bye to the biker couple that manages the building and keep their 1958 Harley-Davidson pan head in the middle of their minuscule living room; good-bye to the exotic dancer whose complete working costume is a dog collar; good-bye to the fifteen gypsies who drive around in a gutted Cadillac with a single fruit crate nailed to the floor on the driver's side; good-bye to the ancient lady downstairs with the cat named LaDeeDa, who raises her paw in greeting when you call her name; good-bye to the fellow we call Green Teeth, and to the lesbians who insist they are "sisters." Good-bye to the insane woman who, among the numerous demented things she says and does, frequently pours urine out her window in the hope that it splashes through the open window of the apartment below. Good-bye to the heroin dealer/junkie who got shot in the head one early summer evening when I was alone and John was in L.A. Good-bye to the elderly Russian immigrant who was dead in her apartment for three days before anyone found her. Good-bye roaches, peeling paint, useless radiator, and the black sludge that spontaneously gurgles up our bathtub drain. And, finally, good-bye to the arsonist who tried to torch our building one night as we all slept blissfully unaware.

1983

John and I move into a larger, much nicer, better-situated apartment. Because it is another studio we (again) sleep in the closet, joking that we are probably the only people left in San Francisco who spend so much time in the closet. We are on the fifth floor, overlooking a sizable, kind of wonderful courtyard. It reminds us of *Rear Window.*

1984

John takes the dog and moves in with friends in the Haight. We are still a couple, we tell people, we just need more room.

I keep the cats. Kali often shares my dinner; her favorite foods, besides chicken and fish, are cantaloupe, butter, cereal with milk, and corn on the cob. She sits close to me when I read, visits me in the bathroom when I bathe, and feigns polite interest when I model new clothes.

Because I tell her everything, she gets a little confused when I am on the phone. She jumps on me, purrs, rubs against me, tries to hold up what she thinks is her end of the conversation.

Sometimes I call her from work—this job is much better than my old job. I like the people, and the hours are quite good—just to imagine her looking up from her extended nap to see if anyone will answer. I don't even have a phone machine to leave a message.

Kali, true to John's prediction, is an extraordinarily beautiful cat. She has seal point Siamese markings accented by a white nose, belly, and socks. Her eyes are a deep, shifting hue of blue. Everyone who meets her remarks on her unusual coloring. As for her personality, she is like having the perfect guest: well-bred, smart, and self-possessed. I've known many cats in my life, but Kali is the hippest by far.

Eventually, I move into a roomy flat in the avenues with my friend Jan. Jan brings home a tiny silver-striped kitten she calls Pooh, and a guy named Jimmy. The duration of Jimmy and Jan's relationship is spent at his flat in North Beach, leaving me in the company of the three cats. Every night they curl up with me on my futon on the floor. I think they think it is nothing more than a giant cat bed and they are graciously allowing me to join them.

1985

This is the year following the year John and I almost got married. We wanted a small ceremony, followed by a sit-down dinner for twenty, at our flat. Kali, J.B., and Pooh are invited, though I am certain only Kali will attend, since she always shows up when we have people over. She doesn't jump on anyone's lap or try to ingratiate herself; she just watches, like some kind of cat journalist.

Then other people got involved with our wedding and soon it was no longer *our* wedding. We allowed ourselves to be talked into a much larger celebration in Los Angeles, instead of insisting on the intimate evening we had planned in San Francisco. While I have always liked attending weddings, I have never been comfortable with the idea of starring in a wedding. Anyway, a few weeks before the grand affair, John and I called the whole thing off. (A consequence of this type of action is that it will be discussed periodically regardless of how often you say, ha ha ha, enough about me, let's talk about you.) Then, for reasons inexplicable even to ourselves, we called the relationship off as well. These were mysterious times for the two of us.

Whywhywhy, asked our families about our abrupt change of heart, and I want to answer it is because, due to the wedding location change, Kali could no longer be a guest. This is what I want to tell people, because it is not as rude as reminding them that some things are too deeply personal to discuss.

1986

I leave the bookkeeping job I have held for the past five and a half years and return to school. John and I didn't stay broken up for very long; we are unmarried and very happy together.

After the spacious city flat, we find ourselves in a tiny, bungalow apartment in Costa Mesa. Our complex has six units and a courtyard outside our front door. It was built in the 1920s, for farm workers, I believe. We are one mile from the beach, and next door to the Hearing Enhancement Center and a mortuary. We tell everyone that, between the Hearing Enhancement Center and the mortuary, our neighbors are very quiet.

This is not strictly true, because during our tenure in that apartment: One of our neighbors tries to commit suicide (unfortunately for him, the entire matter turns comical once the police get involved); this same neighbor, crazy though he is, becomes engaged to an even crazier girl. When he moves out, the clean-cut Christian Scientists move in. They often chat with me but, inexplicably, treat John as if he were invisible. They move out, the cokeheads move in (every time there is a sound outside their door, they whisper anxiously, "Is that the cops?!?"); exit the cokeheads and enter the Loud Family (no explanation necessary). When they leave, a nice immigrant couple of indeterminate nationality moves in. Then someone's parents join them and soon four adults are living in a one-bedroom, five-hundred-square-foot apartment. They appear to be good neighbors, and since they all work multiple jobs and the young couple is also in school full time, I don't think they spend much time together. They are the kind of people who remind you how lazy and truly spoiled you are. The only complaint our absentee landlord has is their habit of hanging their laundry in the living room. The only complaint that the girl next door and I have is that the young man has taken to exercising naked, in a state of arousal, in front of his open window. The front of this particular apartment is about five feet from our bedroom window.

Down the walkway is a creepy single guy who cranks up the volume on his TV as high as it will go when watching pornographic movies. Sometimes, he makes exaggerated noises as he watches. And there is the elderly, unmarried alcoholic couple that lives next door and spends Sunday afternoons, across the room from each other, carrying on lengthy, dispassionate arguments. Once, the woman's grown son came into our apartment, uninvited, when we had dinner guests and proceeded to show us the scars left by a couple of bullet wounds.

There is the robbery and vandalism of the Hearing Enhancement Center, and a pipe bomb that blows a full-size RV out of the alley behind our tiny complex. There is the Fourth of July fire that blazes just yards from our apartment. And the stranger who steals our cans and bottles from the recycling bin outside our kitchen door. The one and only time I catch a glimpse of him is when I am doing my homework at the kitchen table and notice, out of the corner of my eye, a dark, hairy arm with a studded leather bracelet slowly reaching across the open window.

The most surprising tenant is a cat named Finney who could be Kali's brother, their markings are so alike. There are differences: Finney is younger, male, and more aggressive. Kali has a perfect mask across her eyes; Finney's face is white. Kali has never shown much interest in other animals, while Finney is something of a bully. His pugnacious nature is not limited to cats. For example, if you do not pay attention when walking to your car, Finney can give you a fine scare when he leaps out from nowhere and tries to bite off a piece of your flesh. Despite his rough edges, we rather like Finney.

One day, when John and I are parking the car on the street, I notice a cat with seal point Siamese markings, accented with white, lying motionless in the grass and for a second I can't breathe and feel a verging hysteria. I make John look, and it is not Kali but Finney. I am so sad; neither of us wants to tell his owner, and I think, thank God it's not Kali. Then I think, but at some point it will be Kali and what then? I am so shaken, and so relieved that I push the entire matter of a Life Without Kali from my mind and think again about poor, brutish, beautiful Finney and how if you live by the sword, I guess you die by the sword.

1987 & 1988

I spend these years in the graduate writing program at UC Irvine. Even though I am one of the fiction writers, I am still expected to take classes with the doctoral students. This is difficult because I have been out of school for quite a while, and my undergraduate degree is in history, not English. I am introduced to something called critical theory, which is as baffling to me today as it was the first day of class. As with high school algebra, I still have not found a use for it in my daily life. I think it is like this Abstract Expressionist painter once said to a class of art history students: Your theories are good but they mean as much to me as ornithology does to a bird.

In the summer of 1988 I write a short story called "How to Make an American Quilt." I don't plan to show it to anyone. But the hour I finish it my writing teacher, Don Heiney, who never calls me at home, calls me at home, asking if I've written anything over the summer. Not wanting to appear slothful, I say yes, I have been working, and bring my quilt story to him. I am sure he will not like it and I will have to listen to a lecture about what it means to be a serious writer.

I am so wrong. He loves my story and is nothing but encouraging. I tell him thank you, but I am not interested in doing anything with it at this time since I am about to embark on what I can only call The Really Bad Novel. Of course, I don't know that it is really bad yet. You might say, I'm still in that hopeful state.

1989

I finish the writing program in June and turn in The Really Bad Novel as my thesis. I even come up with a really bad title, convincing me that there is some sort of corollary between the length of time it takes to find a title and the quality of the title. It takes me forever to make up this one: *The Still Life, the Landscape, and the Nude.* A publisher's dream, as well as being the perfect beach book. Take it on that long flight to Europe! Lose yourself in it as you commute on the train! *Savor* it.

At the end of September, during one of my incredibly boring daily walks, I unexpectedly envision the quilt story as a novel. I write three drafts in a little less than six months. I tell myself I will never write this quickly again. The novel, it turns out, is identical to the story: identical characters, vignettes, theme, and structure. Everything. It is so simple, so obvious I wonder why it has taken me a year to see it. I feel I have been given a gift.

1990

I pull The Really Bad Novel (the other gift of writing the quilt book) and use *How to Make an American Quilt* as my thesis. I send it to an agent, who gives it to an editor, and my life completely changes.

John and I take a long trip to Europe, where I make a handful of ridiculously expensive calls to Kali at the boardinghouse.

We all move back to San Francisco, city of limited sunshine, into a bigger apartment. Kali and J.B. (our curious Manx who only becomes curiouser as she ages) spend their time chasing the sun around the apartment.

John and I get married for real, in San Francisco, in front of family and one friend. We plan the wedding four days in advance, a kitsch sort of affair, a few steps below an Elvis wedding. Our one friend calls it the Twin Peaks wedding. It is held in a "chapel" in an apartment building that is studded with Christmas lights, with wood paneling covering the floor, walls, and ceiling. There are other lovely decorative touches, including the cash register behind a window, near the entrance with a sign overhead that reads *We do weddings and income tax preparation.* I hear the guests making sniffling noises during the ceremony, and I think, even a cheesy wedding gets to people. This makes me want to cry. It is only after we say I do that I realize everyone was trying not to laugh.

1991

My novel is published. My life continues to change forever.

I am pregnant for most of the year. A lucky aspect of pregnancy is the admonition to stay away from the cat box. When John grumbles about having to clean it, I just say, I would help you but I'm not allowed to, I'm sorry. It occurs to me that many small, petty arguments could be avoided if a person, by advice or decree, simply *couldn't* do as the other person asked.

Of course, I still sleep with the cats, play with them, kiss their little fur. When I consider their hygiene habits I realize this contact is awfully close to communing with the litter box, but I still don't clean it.

Our old futon (we now have a bed) is now on the floor of my office. It's like old times: the cats allowing me to join them on the big cat bed. I am so tired these days. I try to blame my pregnancy, but this exhaustion is limited to the confines of my office. I am writing my second novel and I find I am so hard on myself that I wear myself out. Then I get angry, telling myself I have a lot of nerve to feel anything other than truly fortunate. Then I feel drowsy again and dream about the consequences of getting what you want versus not getting what you want.

1992

The baby is due in February. We buy baby clothes, trying some of them on Kali and J.B. (for anyone sneering, let me say I don't think we are the first). Kali mortified, J.B. resigned.

When the crib is delivered and stored in my office, I have a classic woman/artist/career dilemma moment. Centuries of history threaten to engulf me. I remind myself that John is with me, that he will be, for lack of a better name, a househusband, that he does not feel the crazy anxiety I feel. The truth is I'm scared of teenagers. Throughout my pregnancy I cannot take my eyes off of them.

Kali discovers the crib and claims it. She also claims the car seat and the stroller. I love seeing her sleeping, almost hidden, among the bright-eyed stuffed animals. People exclaim, Oh, but you shouldn't allow cats in the crib! They'll leave dirt! What "dirt" I want to ask. Or they say, You know, if you let them in the crib now, they will continue to jump in it when the baby is born and *steal the baby's breath*. Ooh. Breath thieves. At least they'll finally have a job, I say.

Sam is born, and the cats, those potential baby-killers, cannot get far enough away from him. If he is in the crib, they are not. If he is in the living room, they are in the bedroom. They want nothing to do with him or his breath.

It is important to me that Kali like Sam, but in the end it is J.B. who shyly sleeps on the corner of his blanket as he naps.

We buy our first house, in Portland. It is also the first time I live outside California. It makes me sad to think that Sam will not be growing up in California, and I understand that there will be so many things I will not be able to give my child.

1993

I am sleep obsessed. Sam is one of those sly babies who sleeps through the night within a matter of weeks, only to wake up constantly when he is several months older. I always think about sleep. I lust after sleep. I *dream* about sleep. I hate people who look rested. When I am awakened for the third time and it's only four in the morning, I make future plans to call Sam, when he is an adult, every ninety minutes, all night long, for about six months. I'm supposed to be carrying on a life: as a wife, a friend, a parent, a writer, a homeowner. I should be making new friends, but all I can think about is how all these things interfere with getting enough sleep. I am so cranky I am sometimes surprised that I am still married.

1994

Having a toddler takes up all your time and energy and almost all your love. When I have a clear moment I find myself missing Kali, since I have so little time for her. When I miss Kali, I begin to miss all the things we used to do together. Then I start thinking about what I call My Previous Life. Some of which I miss, and some of which I don't.

Sometimes I miss John, too, even though we promised each other before Sam was born that we would not lose sight of each other. True to my word, I have not allowed Sam to become the center of our universe; sleep is the center of my universe.

1995 & 1996

J.B. dies. She is fifteen. And weird as weird to the end.

Since 1994, Kali is no longer Kali. In her prime she weighed a little over ten pounds, now she's down to five pounds. She's like an old hank of hair that resembles a dirty tufted carpet in a cheap rental unit.

Sam is enamored of his cousin's rat and desperately wants one of his own. He loves placing the rat on his shoulder and walking around with it clinging to his shirt. We tell him he can have one when he is older, but not now. So he has taken to placing little, shrunken Kali on his shoulder, saying, See, Kali's like a rat! Poor Kali, practically blind, nearly deaf, a little senile, spending her days as a surrogate rodent.

She's always at the vet. We medicate her daily. John gives her IVs. She can't sleep through the night and spends it yowling so loud we are all up with her. She eats constantly or nothing at all. She is always thirsty, but for rainwater, not tap water. She might use her box; then again, she might not.

It is so hard, so impossibly hard, Kali's old age.

We know we need to make a decision and the vet is no help. Every time John brings Kali in, I always say good-bye, my heart already aching with loss. Then, he returns with her; I am relieved and guilt-ridden and disappointed to see her.

"Yeah," says John, "the vet thinks Kali might still have a couple more good years." He is grumpy, tired when he says this even though he adored her from the start and I still catch him nuzzling her and whispering her name.

We joke that the vet's remodel must almost be complete; that her kid must be finished with college; that her car is close to being paid off. Then, we say, then she'll tell us what to do.

We know the decision is ours. We can see that Kali is not the old Kali. We can see, even if our son cannot, that Kali is not a rat. Look, it's hard to let go, and letting go of Kali means saying good-bye to so many things: it means we are not the people we once were, living the lives we once lived. It means we are older. It means everything changes, nothing comes back again. It means we foolishly think we can escape nostalgia if we simply refuse to let go.

I think there are roughly three pet phases: the pets we have as children, which die while we are away at college; the pets we take on in college, which die during our shockingly sneaky middle age; the pets we get for our children (which they promise to care for and seldom do), and so begins the cycle again.

Pet love is unconditional love, on both sides. It's as close as some of us can get to a pure love. (This is not to say that it is better than complex human love, since love is love, something without degrees.) Pets will do almost anything for food, which simplifies the entire relationship.

And we love them because they never really know, or understand, how much of who we are, and who we once were, is embodied in them. I think this is why we miss them. I know this is why it is so hard to say good-bye to Kali.

Nancy

BEVERLY DONOFRIO

I met the Dutch on my way home from the general store. She was on her hands and knees in an oval patch of dirt, digging with a hand spade. I'd noticed her before. She had blond hair and braids and didn't seem to fit in at that house with the cop's car in her driveway and the old man in big dark glasses on her porch. The old guy yelled hello at me like a curse every time I walked by. I'd been a New Yorker and I didn't like to *have* to say hello to anybody. I said it back grudgingly and kept my eyes pinned to the sidewalk. Then one day as I passed, the Dutch stood, held out her hand, and said, "Hi, my name's Nancy Exterowicz O'Connor. That's my son Seth, he's four." She indicated a little kid riding a tricycle at the end of the road. Nancy was big and loud. Her eyes seemed to be looking for a joke. "I'm forty-two. I married late in life. I'm not having another." She said that with relief. I'd had a kid too early in life, at seventeen, and had said "I'll never have another" with exactly the same intonation. Also, I'd grown up with a cop car in my driveway because my father was a cop. But I was into finding differences, not similarities, so I didn't mention these things.

"Are you from around here?" I asked her.

"No," she said. "I'm from Cutchogue."

Cutchogue was fifteen miles down the main road.

I might have laughed, but I was not in the mood. I waved hello to her son and went home to the dirty dishes, the books still in boxes, my clean clothes in a heap on the bureau, my dirty clothes in a heap on the floor.

I'd just moved for the fourth time in three years. My son was grown and graduated from college and living his own life back in our old apartment—the one I had left along with my old life and friends to go follow a younger man to the third world. It hadn't worked out. He'd cheated on me with a twenty-four-year-old Mexican virgin, and I'd left him—which was easy. I always left men, and I thought I should be used to it by now. This time, though, the loneliness didn't feel familiar and surmountable, it felt recurring and incurable. I'd broken the city habit and couldn't go back to my old home and friends. I needed to live in the country, and so I'd moved to this village by the sea with nine hundred people, not one of whom I knew. It was close but far enough from the city, and my friends summered here.

I was supposed to be writing a book, but I couldn't. All I could do was fret and obsess. After I'd married at seventeen, I'd vowed never to make that mistake again, so I'd had many men, some adventures, a few stories to tell, and now I was looking at a not-so-distant future as an old biddy. In a few years, high school kids would call me witch, hag, crazy lady. I'd have wild white hair, wear men's pants and leaky rubber boots, kids would throw beer cans at my house.

My mind was too crowded to let the view of the bay exhilarate me with its sapphire beauty. The bike ride past cornfields, beaches, and bullrushes brought tears to my eyes, but everything brought tears to my eyes: an ad in the paper placed by a man wishing his wife of twenty years a happy fortieth birthday, a picture of a smiling dog up for adoption.

My friends arrived for the summer. There were invitations to beach parties and dinners, but I couldn't be witty and friendly and smile. Sometimes I said no, even though to refuse an invitation indicated a lack of social backbone and my roots in the lower classes. The summer ended. Everybody left. The sun went down at four-thirty, and my heart grew so heavy I couldn't get out of bed.

But sometimes, through vanity and sheer force of will, I managed to drag myself to aerobics. I always said hello to the women there but rarely talked, and so I was surprised when at Christmastime a woman named Sam invited me to her house for a party. Her husband was a commercial fisherman and would be gone for two weeks. It was an all-women's party. I made myself go although I knew it would be painful. Everyone there would have Farah Fawcett hair and wear turquoise and pink, aviator glasses, and acid-washed jeans. They would love *The Bridges of Madison County*. They would all eat dinner at 5:30, have heart-shaped everythings, and say "ain't" like my parents. I'd thought that I'd traveled far in my life but I'd just circled back home. Ah, now there was another poisonous thought to add to my arsenal.

Sam and her friend Amy, also from aerobics, were in the

kitchen putting quesadillas into the oven. They asked me if I'd
like an eggnog or a margarita. I'd been staying away from booze
because it only made me more depressed, but I needed a drink
to walk into the living room, where I could see there were a
half-dozen women sitting around its edges in kitchen chairs, all
wearing wedding rings. I took a margarita.

Nancy Exterowicz was in a corner, her ankles crossed, her
hands in her lap, managing to look at the same time prim and
uncomfortable. She was wearing a calf-length denim skirt and a
white blouse on which she'd sewn a cobalt blue bolt of lightning
in sequins.

I sat in the chair next to hers. Someone asked Sam what her
husband had gone fishing for, and Sam said, "Tuna," as she
passed a bowl of Brazil nuts that had been glazed with something very sweet and delicious.

I remarked that I hadn't realized fishing was still a viable industry in Chester, and Sam said that there were still a few boats
left. Karen, a heavy woman with white hair and blinking lights
on her sweater, said that Chester used to be a whaling town and
the men had been gone for two-year stretches. "Every man in
the town, gone. The grades in the elementary school skipped
every two years."

"Wish my old man would go off for two years," said Amy.
She'd put on her baseball cap.

"Achh. They're all pains in the ass," Nancy Exterowicz
summed up. "I never wanted to get married. I told him to pull
out."

"Your husband's a cop?" one of the women asked.

"A *marine* policeman. It means he drives a big boat and
doesn't do shit. We had rats running on the ceiling."

"The ceiling?" somebody gasped.

"You couldn't see them. They were up above. But you could hear them like a highway. Mr. Rod and Gun Club wouldn't get out of the bed to shoot'm. I was the one who had to do it. I woke him up, dangled one over his face."

I smelled marijuana. Sam was about to pass a joint. Then I noticed a tiny cut-crystal vase next to the platter of Christmas cookies on the coffee table. It contained six joints.

"I brought some," Nancy said. "Homegrown." She pulled a pint-sized Ball jar from her bag and began to roll.

"You grew it?" I asked.

"Yeah," she said. "It's sinsemilla. You weed out the males."

I was beginning to remember what it was about my hometown that I had missed all these years. My wild high school girlfriends and the comfort that can be found in man-bashing. I hadn't smoked in over three years, but I took a sip of pot.

The party moved to the kitchen, where somebody opened a bottle of tequila and poured shots. "Here's to Christmas," somebody said. "Fuck Christmas," Amy said. "Here's to spring." We drank. Another round was poured. "Aren't you two neighbors?" Amy asked me and Nancy, who was standing at the opposite counter, lifting hot clams off a cookie sheet with her fingers.

"Yeah," we said looking at each other.

"How do you like that Curt?" She was talking about the old man on her porch. She reminisced about the time last summer a lost kitten had climbed up under her car and yowled all night long. In the morning, Curt had stood at the edge of their porch and yelled, "Shut up! Shut up! Shut that damned cat up." I went over to see if I could help coax the cat out, and Curt yelled, "Get my shotgun. I'm going to shoot it."

"You can't see," Nancy had reminded him. He had cataracts.

"You aim and I'll pull the trigger," he said.

We laughed at the memory. "Pull the trigger, my ass," Nancy said.

"Foot-long dong," said Karen with the blinking sweater. She was the woman who wrote the column about our village in the local paper. "They say once they made a bet at the general store how many quarters it would take to measure his dick. He laid it right on the counter."

"No! How many?" we wanted to know.

"Thirteen," she said.

"No!"

Later, I was too drunk to drive, but Nancy claimed she had the constitution of a horse and could drive to Alaska if she had to, so she drove me. In the car she said, "I should have helped you. You kept carrying all those boxes." She was referring to the day I'd moved. "They were books, right? I always felt guilty for that. Did you read all those books?"

"No. Well, most."

"You must be smart. I'm a DP."

"DP?"

"Dumb Polack. I stayed back in the third grade."

Nancy said I should come over anytime I saw the lights on at her shed. That meant she was accepting visitors. I hadn't noticed there was a shed.

The next day I awoke with an anvil hangover. I read the Sunday *Times* and thought about how I was a snob and wrong about everything. What kind of person had I become? I knew nothing except that I knew nothing, and that life was going on all around me while I was living in a tomb. I thought I should at least walk out into my yard, cut a bow of evergreen, and put it in a vase, but I didn't.

One night I did look for Nancy's shed from my window but saw nothing. A few nights later I put on my jacket and stepped outside. I walked down toward the dead end, and sure enough, behind her house was a shed, like a doll's house, silhouetted in Christmas lights, blinking on and off.

When she opened the door, my heart started to race as though I'd inhaled a stimulant. The walls were covered every inch with Nancy's collections: Dutch shoes, cow figurines, pigs, cherries, tomatoes, turkeys, hearts, butterflies, made of glass and metal and wood and wax, shells, bones, teeth, and feathers. Fishing poles crisscrossed the beams up above and from them hung dozens of bunches of flowers she'd grown, then dried for making wreaths. She sat at a bench and went on twisting wire around evergreen boughs, making Christmas wreaths. Her fingertips were bandaged and protruding from gloves with the fingers cut off (there was no warmth in the shed besides what was produced by a small portable heater). Muddy Waters was on her tape deck, incense was burning, and she worked by candlelight. I took a seat.

Soon, Nancy was calling every day and saying, "Just checking in." She dropped by unannounced, burst into my kitchen with her sunny big blond energy, and wiped the crumbs off the counter, watered my plants, straightened the crooked picture, as much to help me as because she is constitutionally unable to sit still. She told me her nickname was the Dutch because she wanted to be a duchess and she collected Dutch shoes. She nicknamed me Bundala, short for Bundle of Love, because Bundle of Love is what I called my cat. One morning I walked out to get the paper and discovered that she and her son had built a snow woman on my front lawn. She had big breasts with chestnuts for nipples. I yelled, "You can't show breasts in my front yard. It's obscene. Why didn't you build it in your own front yard?"

"'Cause we wanted to see the Bundala go crazy," she said.

Seth laughed. "Yeah. We wanted to make you mad."

"The school bus goes by here," I continued.

"We'll cover'm up." Nancy brought a madras scarf from her house and made it into a bikini top. As soon as the sun fell each night, she pulled one side of it down and exposed a breast, which made it more obscene. In the morning, before the school bus drove by, she pulled it back up.

One morning in the spring of that year, I awoke to an eerie lemony color lighting up my room. It was only six-thirty. I'd never seen anything like it. I sat up in bed and looked out the window. The whole world was cast in this startling yellow light. My chest filled, not only from the weird beauty of it but because I knew Nancy would be seeing it too.

Nancy did beadwork, she made quilts, she knitted, she crocheted, she built things out of wood, rewired lamps, soldered, carved, rearranged furniture and pictures and knickknacks. She cooked and cleaned, and in the summer she planted and weeded, built arbors, clammed, scalloped, and went crabbing. She'd been the oldest of five girls with a father who managed a bowling alley bar and was never home, so Nancy became the man of the house. A real man in my house would have been nice, but I was through letting myself wilt without one. I would be strong and capable and active like Nancy. It wasn't a decision really. It was more that Nancy had rubbed off. She gave me plants she'd dug from her yard and taught me how to garden, giving me the greatest gift I have ever received, the experience of feeling the sun on my neck and the wind in my hair as my hands reached into the earth.

In a way, Nancy taught me to say yes, and I taught her to say no. The wealthy old lady who lived beside her, whom Nancy hardly knew and didn't like, expected Nancy to come by twice a day, unpaid, to put drops in her eyes. Nancy cleaned houses for a living and was so strong and so fast she did the work of two people in half the time, yet got paid five dollars less than scale. "You have to value yourself more," I told her.

By July, we were taking a bike ride every evening, sometimes as late as midnight. We'd pedal and pedal, and Nancy would complain. Her husband called her a Dumb Polack. He said she didn't have a brain in her head. He commanded her, "Change the channel. . . . Get me a beer. . . . Shut your mouth." Seth was beginning to pick up his father's attitude, and Nancy was concerned. And she was getting sick and tired. She did all the housework, the cooking, the cleaning. She mowed the lawn, gardened, and shoveled in winter. She paid for all the food, and all he paid for was the utilities. Rent was free because Curt, the old man on the porch, owned their house and was her husband's uncle. The deal had been that if they cared for Curt, they'd inherit the house after he died. Curt had separate living quarters but they shared a bathroom on the first floor. Curt often missed the toilet and it was up to Nancy to mop up. When they first moved in, right after they married, her husband had a bathroom built upstairs. The plumbing had been installed, and all that needed to be done was for her husband to take the toilet out of the box and fasten it in place.

"Six years, and it's still in the box." Nancy pedaled harder. "He comes home last night and throws his dinner in the garbage because it's leftovers. Then he goes up to his room and bolts the door. Never said two words to his son." His room was the attic he'd had built into his own huge bedroom, where he'd installed the 27-inch TV Nancy's mother had given her for her fortieth birthday.

I pedaled harder. "Tell him to cook for himself," I said. "When he tells you to get him a beer, say no."

"My mother says I should keep my big mouth shut and do what he says. My mother says I provoke him. My mother says—"

I said, "Don't listen to your mother."

"What am I supposed to do? She calls me every day."

"Tell her you don't feel like discussing it, and if she continues you'll have to hang up. You have to train mothers," I told her.

She thought that was a riot. She told her mother I said it. Her mother has hated me ever since.

Little by little over the next year Nancy began to stop taking crap. She went out when she felt like it, and when her husband forbade her to have her friends in the house, we went there anyway.

Then it got dangerous. First, he cut up the quilt she'd been hand-stitching for three years. Next he hacked up a dress form and threw it out the window. Nancy loved her possessions, and attacking them physically was the same as attacking her, which was his next step. She was talking on the phone to a friend and when he told her to hang up she wouldn't. He grabbed it from her hand, hit her over the head with it, and then when she kicked him, he threw her through the front door. She ran to my house and called the police. But her husband's a cop. When the police arrived at her house, she stepped out my door and began to walk over. The cop yelled in a disgusted tone, "Get back in that house. I'll call you when I'm ready."

Her husband came out and the two of them laughed on her lawn for a half hour. When the cop finally came over, he told her she ought to watch her mouth and be more careful not to provoke her husband. She had her son to consider.

We found a battered women's center and they counseled her to call the state police the next time, which she did. Then she got an order of protection, which meant that he was to refrain from violence, but not that he had to leave the house. Nancy had no money to move herself. She began to save every penny and then filed for custody papers so when she did move out, her husband couldn't claim she'd stolen their son. These papers had to be served by a third party, and so I served them.

He looked at them and snarled, "Put them over there." He indicated the top of the washer.

I hesitated for a second, wondering if it was required that he take the papers from my hand. "And get out of here. Get out, you fucking dyke. You'd better hope I never see you set foot in—"

I saw the snarl, I heard the hate, I felt the contempt, and I lost it. "Are you threatening me?" I was up on my toes.

"Don't you ever"—we were chest-to-chest—"fucking ever"—I was jabbing my finger an inch from his face—"threaten me. Ever again. You FUCK." I was throbbing with adrenaline. My eyes were bugging out. If I had had a gun I would have killed him. I was out of my mind with rage, but then something happened. I saw a flicker of fear in his eyes. The rage drained from me and I deflated. He was a bully who'd been bullied back. A coward. I felt sorry for him. I dropped my gaze and left.

Things got worse. A few more orders of protection were issued. Nancy was looking older. Her eyes were going hard. She couldn't relax by doing work with her hands anymore, so she did jigsaw puzzles instead. Inevitably, she'd have a half-dozen pieces left to place and her husband would walk into the room, grin at her, grab a handful of the puzzle and toss the pieces across the room. Nancy kept her cool, as her counselor advised. She swept the old puzzle into a box and started another. Nancy was waiting for the last laugh.

She found a little house that needed a lot of work but cost only four hundred a month. It was three miles down the main road. She and I and her friends Mo and Amy kept it a secret. Then, as planned, when her husband went to visit his family for three days over Thanksgiving, Nancy, Mo, Amy, and I emptied her house. Every stick. She took the washer, the dryer, the stove, and the refrigerator. She even took the compost pile. She'd accumulated so many collectibles from tag sales, which were like members of her own family to her, that it took us every waking minute of those three days to move them.

Her mother stopped by in the middle of it and fretted. "All this junk, Nancy. Oh, my God. Where you going to put it? You're crazy, you'd better throw it away." Mo and Amy and I looked glumly at each other as Nancy stood up, walked to the middle of the room, did a tap dance, and fell to the floor, her arms spread like a cross, and laughed. Even her mother had to laugh. But only for a second. Then she said, "Why don't you wear a rubber band on your wrist and when you feel yourself getting like that snap it."

"I'd rather snap my clit," Nancy said.

"Your what?" said her mother.

By sunset on Sunday the house was empty. We didn't know exactly when her husband was due back, but Nancy had to risk it. She took the boxes of ruined puzzles she'd saved and strew the pieces around the house, on the floors of every room and on the stairways. She poured cement with puzzle pieces mixed in it down the pipe for the toilet that had never been installed, and then just before we left, she put puzzle pieces on the blades of the ceiling fan. When her husband thought he'd finally seen the end of them and he turned on the fan that summer, puzzles would rain down on his head.

And so Nancy moved. She's not my neighbor anymore, but she is my sister. She still stops by unannounced. Her favorite time is around dinner when I'm in my kitchen cooking. She stands at the door. Just stands there, so that when I turn around I'll see a body at my door, jump a foot, and scream, which I never fail to do, no matter how many times she does it. Then she falls into the kitchen, on her back, her arms out like a cross, and laughs.

Eli Tannen

(Photo by Laurie Leifer)

DEBORAH TANNEN

INCHING

"You loved your grandmother so much," my mother says, talking of her own mother, who lived with us until she died. "When you were little, you'd walk along and hold her hand. Mimi would run ahead, but you always stayed with her. You had such patience."

This praise I hear as an indictment, because I know how wrong she is. I was not patient. I held my grandmother's hand and inched along beside her because I didn't know how to escape the expectation that I would. I resented being the chosen one. Like a pony tethered to a post, I envied Mimi, my middle sister, two years older, who was not thus bound.

I have always felt I hid a terrible secret: I loved my grandmother, but not as much, or as completely, as the little girl in my mother's stories. I did love things about her. I loved to look through the old pictures she kept in a shoe box in the room that was hers in our big old house. One by one, I'd pull out small discolored photographs of people and ask her who they were. And I loved to comb her long thin hair, not entirely gray even when she was in her eighties. Then it was her turn to be patient, and I think she really was. But I also harbored nuggets of resentment; being leashed to her pace while she walked was one.

It is years since I've thought of those slow walks along the uneven squares of Brooklyn pavement, stony corners of pebble-specked concrete sidewalk jutting out. I think of them now because I find myself inching along beside an old person again. But this time I do feel patient—not only because I am older and slower myself, no longer burning with the fever of a child's energy, but because this time I am truly burning with the fever of love. The person I am walking slowly beside is my father.

DADDY

My childhood, in my mind, is an endless train of days spent with my mother, missing my father. My mother is a continuous arc; my father is a series of snapshots that I take with me wherever I go.

In one, I am walking along the Brooklyn street of my childhood holding my father's hand. When my father holds my hand, he has to slow his pace to my little girl's steps. I love the hard rough skin of his huge calloused hand, a big safe house around my fragile little one.

My father rides the subway home from work in Manhattan to the Cortelyou Road station in Brooklyn, then walks the twenty minutes from the station to our house. On the lucky days when he comes home while it is still light, Mimi and I wait for him to appear at the end of the street. When we see his tall thin shape taking form, we run to him. He lifts us up, one by one, and holds us in his arms, then sets us down and walks the last half block with us—a little girl fastened to the end of each arm.

If he arrives home before we go to bed, Daddy tucks us in. When my blanket is a jumble, he stands at the end of my bed, takes the blanket by its corners, spreads it between the enormous expanse of his outstretched arms, and gives it a great shake, making it fly in the air above the bed and come to rest over me, smooth and comforting. As Mimi and I lie in our beds, he tells us stories he made up himself, in which we are the heroes who save the town from dragons. Our favorites are "stories with actions." In telling one of these, he moves around our beds, acting the story out, rushing, at key points, toward our mock-scared, upturned, laughing faces.

But most nights he comes home late after working overtime as a cutter in the garment district, then putting in more hours at what I know as his "being active" in the Brownsville–East New York Liberal Party. I beg in vain to be allowed to wait up so I can see him before I go to sleep.

My sister Naomi is not in these pictures. Eight years older than I, she must have been in her own world of friends.

DADDY AT HOME AND AWAY

My father leaves the house before anyone else wakes up in the morning. He sometimes eats breakfast in the candy store on Coney Island Avenue, around the corner from our house. This is the same store that I walk to when I want to buy whatever it is the neighborhood kids crave that season—hula hoops or yo-yos or slinky balloons—or, if Mimi or I have an upset stomach, the pure Coke syrup that amazingly is considered medicine. When I go into the store during the flat daytime hours, I look with awe at the round counter stools, upholstered in red leather with silver chrome encircling their sides, because I know that my father sat on one of them, eating fried eggs and bacon while my family slept. That he wakes up so early seems to me heroic; that he has breakfast at the candy store seems exotic and adds to the magic of the store.

The strongest presence that I feel in the house is my father's absence. It clings to his places and possessions. One is his dresser: he has built dividers into the top drawer so his socks are lined up in compact little lumps sorted by color. Another is his desk, which he built himself. It has row on row of little compartments just the right size for what they hold: four wide shelves for different kinds of paper, tiny compartments for paper clips and rubber bands, vertical dividers for the small slips of scratch paper he makes by cutting up sheets of outdated stationery. The cellar is where he builds these things. His tools line the walls, hanging from nails. One wall is covered with narrow shelves on which baby food jars hold nails and screws, sorted by size.

My favorite object in the house is an old black typewriter with yellowing keys rimmed in tarnished silver. I spend hours typing letters to my father, telling him what happened to me during the day and laying out my grievances against my mother. I can't have any grievances against him, because he isn't there.

My father is home, working in the cellar. I sit on the steps and watch. He asks why I don't go outside and play, but playing is dull beside the excitement of being with him. Times I am allowed to enter his world stand out like sentences highlighted in yellow. I love helping him stuff envelopes for political mailings (line up the flaps with glue exposed and swipe a wet sponge over six at a time) or going from house to house distributing political leaflets.

My father is working at his desk. I enter the room and stand beside him. He hasn't heard me come in, and he doesn't notice that I am standing there. Without thinking, I do something to get his attention: I squirt him in the face with my water gun. He erupts, roaring like a frightened tiger and shaking suddenly with a great shudder of fright. Terrified, I dart out of the room, down the stairs, and onto the first landing of the staircase, where I crouch, waiting to run down the rest of the way if he is angry at me. He appears at the top of the stairs, looming like a tower, and laughs, his laugh opening like his arms, inviting me to run against his chest and into his huge hug. With his arms and his hug and his laugh reassuring, he apologizes for scaring me.

I have a splinter in my finger, and I want my father to take it out. If I give my finger over to my mother, she will jab at it with a straight pin; it will hurt, and I don't trust her to get the whole splinter out. When my father takes out a splinter, he elaborately sets up an operating table: lays out alcohol, matches, pin, tweezers, and a razor blade. He holds the point of the pin to a burning match, then sterilizes both the pin and the razor blade with alcohol. Then he turns to the operation. Methodically, he shaves off thin layers of skin with the blade, so carefully that it is painless. The razor blade—redolent of masculine ritual—is a dangerous instrument that only he can be trusted to wield. When he exposes the splinter, he loosens it with the pin, then lifts it out with the tweezers. It never hurts. I insist on leaving the splinter in place until he gets home.

TRANSFORMATION

Our lives change when I am in junior high school.

My father is leaving for work at what seems a languorous hour: 8:30 A.M. Wearing a suit, he is standing at his dresser, transferring to designated pockets the items he emptied onto the top right corner of his dresser the night before. He is going to the office where he practices law.

My father has a law degree and a master's degree in law. But he graduated from law school in 1930, when there was no work for lawyers. In 1958, twenty-eight years after graduating from law school, he is finally rewarded for the years of evenings and weekends spent working for the Liberal Party. He has been appointed Assistant Counsel to the Workmen's Compensation Board. But after only six months, Nelson Rockefeller, a Republican, is elected governor, and my father loses his job. This time, however, he doesn't go back to the factory. He begins practicing workmen's compensation law.

And I begin going to high school in Manhattan. Now I too take the long walk to the subway station. But I still don't see my father in the morning. Now I'm the one who leaves the house before he or anyone else wakes up.

When my father goes to work in an office, the calluses that formed on his palms over the years of handling the cutting machine and giant shears gradually wear off, and his hands turn soft. I miss the calluses that made his hands rough and hard.

. . .

My father is standing at the door. We are in the apartment he and my mother moved to after I went away to college. I am home during a break. He is asking where his nail file is. Careless and chaotic, I am always losing things. When I want something, I know I can find it among his possessions. This time I have taken his nail file, which is always lying at the outer edge of the second shelf in his desk, to the right. It is a dependable metal file, slightly bent because he has had it all my life. Finding it gone, he knows I am the culprit. He stands and confronts me, not in anger, but in quiet exasperation, and although he does not reprimand me, but simply asks where his nail file is, I feel found out. I do not remember where I left it. Standing there, not angry, he looms over me like an implacable judgment.

My father's orderliness is a foundation I can count on, and his height is a bulwark against chaos. When I was a little girl, he seemed, at 6 feet, to be as tall as the Empire State Building. Because of this, very tall men fill me with awe, making the backs of my thighs tingle as if I were standing at a precipice.

MY FATHER AT A REMOVE

I have been asked to write a piece for the theater. Because I have published a book about the conversational styles of women and men, I am certain they expect an amusing dialogue that dramatizes misunderstandings typical of couples. I have been staring at the computer screen for days, writing and deleting sentences.

At the same time, I write a poem about a trip my husband and I made with my parents—a trip to Warsaw, where my father was born and lived until he was twelve. Standing on the street where he played as a child, my father described the world he grew up in. The outlines of his childhood that I had always known took on life. (His father died when he was six, but his mother had thrown her husband out when my father was two, so he never knew his father.) I send the poem to a friend to whom I also complain that my attempts to write a play are leading nowhere. He comments that the poem sounds like the beginning of a play. The next day I start writing a play based o ı our trip to Warsaw. It juxtaposes my father's memories of his hildhood in Poland with my memories of my childhood with him.

I read the play to my parents. I am sitting on the couch in the living room of their apartment in Westchester, and my mother sits beside me on the couch. My father sits on an upholstered chair at the far end of the couch. When I finish reading the play, my mother, weeping, throws her arms around me, telling me how wonderful the play, and I, are. My father begins speaking about something else. I am stunned. I have written a play about his life, and he doesn't seem to care. The next day he writes me a letter telling me how moved he was, and explaining that he changed the subject because he didn't want to show his emotion. He also makes a comment that captures the point of the play: "I had no father," he says, "but I didn't miss him. You had a father, but you missed him."

THE TELEPHONE

From the time I left my parents' house for college, when I called home it was my mother I spoke to. After we'd spoken for a long time, she'd say, "Your father wants to talk to you." I'd feel a little leap of excitement, almost as if a boy I had a crush on finally called. My father would get on the phone and say, almost at once, "Well, it was nice talking to you." "Wait," I'd say, with a panic-like sense that something I really wanted was slipping away. "You haven't talked to me yet." "We'll talk when we see each other," he'd say. "There's no point in making the phone company rich." He'd gotten on the phone just to get me off.

When I call home now it is not much changed. If my father answers, he quickly says, "I'll tell Mother you're on the phone. She'll be so happy to hear from you." He calls to her and she picks up an extension. It's not long before I realize I haven't heard his voice for a while. "Where's Daddy?" I ask. "He hung up," she says. My father isn't interested in the things my mother and I talk about: what relatives and friends are up to, what they said.

If my mother answers the phone, she and I talk for a long time. I finally say I have to go because I am tired or have something I must do, but then I add, "Can I say hello to Daddy?" "Do you have time?" she asks. "I thought you were tired." "I am," I say, "but I just want to say hello." One time she makes a joke: "Well, I don't know. If you're nice, maybe you can."

There is one situation in which my father will talk on the phone: if I call when my mother is not home, and I ask him about his past. I delight in these conversations, but my mother doesn't. She accuses him: "You only want to talk about people who are dead."

When I hear my father's voice on the phone, that rush of excitement is still there. I feel a lightness in the air, a giddiness. He is always cheerful and funny. My mother's aging has been nearly invisible: at eighty-five she does not move like an old person, and she has developed her very first ache: a sore shoulder. My father has suffered pain his whole life, from dental work, from a perforated ulcer, from arthritis, from surgery as recently as last year. He has trouble getting up and trouble walking. But he never lets on if he is in pain. When he was immobilized with excruciating and relentless pain from sciatica running the entire length of his left leg, from hip to toe, I asked, "How are you doing?" He answered, "Wonderful! The whole right side of my body doesn't hurt at all!"

MY SISTER'S FATHER

To write another play about my father, I decide to interview my family about their perceptions of him. I ask my oldest sister, Naomi, what she remembers about Daddy when she was a child.

"He used to toss ideas back and forth to me the way other fathers play ball," Naomi says. "He used to have debates with me where he would pick an issue and take the hard-to-defend side that he obviously didn't believe in. For example, we once discussed slavery, and he took the side that slavery was good so I could take the other position, the right one. I never felt put down. You know, some fathers, when they play competitive games with their kids, they like to win. But I never thought it was competitive. It was fun. He was teaching me to think and to argue."

When my father tossed ideas like baseballs back and forth with Naomi, I must have been a baby, or not yet born. Yet I hear her as if I were deliberately left out, cheated. I recall having political discussions with him when I was older, but it was over dinner, with others present. And I recall that I loved to have him give me words to spell. But I have in mind only one specific occasion when he did this, as we were walking along Coney Island Avenue. I was accompanying him on an errand, so my presence was an afterthought, not the main point.

I can't imagine my father having time to sit and talk to me when I was little. Is this simply because I was the youngest of three? He couldn't be alone with one of three as he was when there was only one. But this can't be the whole story. Naomi was born during the Depression. During those years he either worked for the WPA—which wasn't full time—or held jobs with normal hours, which gave him evenings and weekends at home. When I was conceived, the family was living in Providence, Rhode Island, where my father had a civil service job. But my mother wasn't happy living in Rhode Island and wanted to be nearer her family when the baby came, so they moved back to New York City. As a stopgap measure, my father returned to working in a factory while he entered politics in the hope of receiving a political appointment to a position for which his law degrees qualified him. The thirteen years that it took for this to happen were the first thirteen years of my life. Perhaps his absence was my punishment for setting those years in motion with my birth.

Naomi says, "My earliest memories are of his being nurturing, maybe because I heard about it. I'm astounded at how much child care he did. Because he worked all day! He would come home from work at the end of the day and wash my diapers. He knew it was twelve diapers. Every night he'd come home and wash the twelve diapers. And he used to iron my little dresses. He remembers that he knew how to iron the puffed sleeves.

"My earliest memory," Naomi continues, "is living in Bensonhurst. I guess I was about four. I hurt myself. I fell, skinned my knee or my arm, and I remember a side door to a building, maybe to our apartment, and Daddy brought me inside through that door and bandaged it for me."

My memory of splinters shrinks to a paltry shadow beside Naomi's accounts of his ministries. He was so present in her young life, in searing contrast to his absence in mine, that listening to her causes almost physical pain.

DADDY'S CHILDREN

I ask my father what he remembers of our childhoods. He says, "I only remember little incidents. One is when Naomi had chicken pox. She must have been a year and a half? Two years? And the doctor warned us, 'If you scratch, you're left with scars. So you mustn't scratch.' And she was suffering. She said, 'Itch me, Mommy! Itch me!' And we said, 'No, you mustn't.' And she was such a good girl, she didn't scratch. Now they have cream. I put on cortisone, and it stops the itch. It's amazing. Every time I have an itch and I put on the cortisone and it stops the itch, I think of Naomi."

I ask, "Do you think it was different when Mimi and I had chicken pox?" His answer is straightforward: "I don't remember." The explanation is self-evident, but I say it anyway: "Maybe by the time we had it, you weren't around so much." He concedes the obvious: "I was too busy." But he adds, "I was earning better. And it's a good thing."

I ask for more memories, and one after another, he gives me

Naomi. "She must have been five or six. She was playing with these older girls, and there were a few stairs in the back, and I gathered a big pile of hay, and the bigger kids started jumping—not with the feet down but with the tushy down. And Naomi followed them, and one jump, she missed it, and she hit with her tushy on the concrete. And I got terribly scared—she could have fractured her spine. I brought her into the house. And she was all right. But I was more careful after that."

Naomi's triumph cannot be challenged. She is the native citizen in my father's memory. I am the resident alien.

DADDY OUT OF REACH

Here is another bit of evidence my mother often provides of how much I loved her mother: my grandmother's death when I was seven was one of the great traumas of my childhood. She is right that I was horrified by my grandmother's death. I can see myself back then in the Brooklyn street outside our house, standing beside my father's black Buick with its three chrome notches on the side fender, stunned that children were still thoughtlessly playing after such a dreadful thing had happened. But, as I recall the dread I felt, it wasn't the loss of my grandmother that shook me. It was the fact of death: that I could go blithely off to school in the morning, unsuspecting, and return to find a person gone—vanished, poof, never again to be seen on the earth. If it could happen to my grandmother, then it could also happen to the person I really loved: my father.

I had a fear that I knew was trivial but was terrifying nonetheless. When my teacher told us to look up something in the encyclopedia, I often asked my father instead. He knew everything. If he died, I thought, I'd have to look things up in books, like everyone else. The prospect left me desolate.

Years ago I had this dream: I'm at my own birthday party. My father is there, but he's suspended about two feet off the ground, with his head near the ceiling. I don't know what he's doing up there; he doesn't seem to be doing anything, just floating in his own world. I can't reach him, and he doesn't hear me or see me. I desperately try to make contact with him, but he's stuck up there and I can't get him to come down.

Around the same time, I had a dream about Bob, the man I was seeing then: a tall thin man with prematurely gray hair. He was riding a horse, and something terrible had happened to him. Finally, the horse, with him on it, was led back to the stable. Bob's leg had been hurt, and he was dazed. As they took him down from the horse, I rushed over, trying to help. But he couldn't see me, and he couldn't hear anything I was saying. I was desperate to make sure he was okay, but he was oblivious of me.

INCHING

I am visiting my parents in Florida, relieved to be away from the chaos of my own office, where every surface is covered with papers and nothing is where it should be. This small, sun-filled apartment was never home to me, and the furnishings are not the ones I grew up with, yet the order my father has created in these scaled-down rooms makes me feel like I have come home. His desk is a white laminate surface built in against a wall. He has added plastic trays with tiny compartments into which he has sorted tacks, safety pins, paper clips and rubber bands—all ordered by size. Three dispensers perfectly aligned hold three different types of tape. In his closet, over the shelves, he has hammered in nails on which to hang his hats.

My father is recovering from bypass surgery in his leg. I walk with him on the catwalk that runs along the building to the elevator. How strange, I think, life is to bring things round to this: my father, who never walked up stairs but sent them sailing behind him two at a time, inching along.

I am grateful to time for having slowed him down. My father old has time for me as my father young did not. The skin of his hand is stiff, as it was when I was little, only now the hardness is not from calluses but from age: the skin dried, the muscle between thumb and palm shrunk concave from a pinched nerve. If I am holding his hand, he can't disappear, run away, recede. I feel as if, were I to let go of his hand, he would fall, as he does in my dreams: thudding to the ground. So I hold his hand, hold him in my hand.

Gus Oldham

INSPIRED ECCENTRICITY:
SARAH AND GUS OLDHAM

BELL HOOKS

There are family members you try to forget and ones that you always remember, that you can't stop talking about. They may be dead—long gone—but their presence lingers and you have to share who they were and who they still are with the world. You want everyone to know them as you did, to love them as you did.

All my life I have remained enchanted by the presence of my mother's parents, Sarah and Gus Oldham. When I was a child they were already old. I did not see that then, though. They were Baba and Daddy Gus, together for more than seventy years at the time of his death. Their marriage fascinated me. They were strangers and lovers—two eccentrics who created their own world.

More than any other family members, together they gave me a worldview that sustained me during a difficult and painful childhood. Reflecting on the eclectic writer I have become, I see in myself a mixture of these two very different but equally powerful figures from my childhood. Baba was tall, her skin so white and her hair so jet black and straight that she could have easily "passed" denying all traces of blackness. Yet the man she married was short and dark, and sometimes his skin looked like the color of soot from burning coal. In our childhood the fireplaces burned coal. It was bright heat, luminous and fierce. If you got too close it could burn you.

Together Baba and Daddy Gus generated a hot heat. He was a man of few words, deeply committed to silence—so much so that it was like a religion to him. When he spoke you could hardly hear what he said. Baba was just the opposite. Smoking an abundance of cigarettes a day, she talked endlessly. She preached. She yelled. She fussed. Often her vitriolic rage would heap itself on Daddy Gus, who would sit calmly in his chair by the stove, as calm and still as the Buddha sits. And when he had enough of her words, he would reach for his hat and walk.

Neither Baba nor Daddy Gus drove cars. Rarely did they ride in them. They preferred walking. And even then their styles were different. He moved slow, as though carrying a great weight; she with her tall, lean, boyish frame moved swiftly, as though there was never time to waste. Their one agreed-upon passion was fishing. Though they did not do even that together. They lived close but they created separate worlds.

In a big two-story wood frame house with lots of rooms they constructed a world that could contain their separate and distinct personalities. As children one of the first things we noticed about our grandparents was that they did not sleep in the same room. This arrangement was contrary to everything we understood about marriage. While Mama never wanted to talk about their separate worlds, Baba would tell you in a minute that Daddy Gus was nasty, that he smelled like tobacco juice, that he did not wash enough, that there was no way she would want him in her bed. And while he would say nothing nasty about her, he would merely say why would he want to share somebody else's bed when he could have his own bed to himself, with no one to complain about anything.

I loved my granddaddy's smells. Always, they filled my nostrils with the scent of happiness. It was sheer ecstasy for me to be allowed into his inner sanctum. His room was a small Van Gogh–like space off from the living room. There was no door. Old-fashioned curtains were the only attempt at privacy. Usually the curtains were closed. His room reeked of tobacco. There were treasures everywhere in that small room. As a younger man Daddy Gus did odd jobs, and sometimes even in his old age he would do a chore for some needy lady. As he went about his work, he would pick up found objects, scraps. All these objects would lie about his room, on the dresser, on the table near his bed. Unlike all other grown-ups he never cared about children looking through his things. Anything we wanted he gave to us.

Daddy Gus collected beautiful wooden cigar boxes. They held lots of the important stuff—the treasures. He had tons of little diaries that he made notes in. He gave me my first wallet, my first teeny little book to write in, my first beautiful pen, which did not write for long, but it was still a found and shared treasure. When I would lie on his bed or sit close to him, sometimes just standing near, I would feel all the pain and anxiety of my troubled childhood leave me. His spirit was calm. He gave me the unconditional love I longed for.

"Too calm," his grown-up children thought. That's why he had let this old woman rule him, my cousin BoBo would say. Even as children we knew that grown-ups felt sorry for Daddy Gus. At times his sons seemed to look upon him as not a "real man." His refusal to fight in wars was another sign to them of weakness. It was my grandfather who taught me to oppose war. They saw him as a man controlled by the whims of others, by this tall, strident, demanding woman he had married. I saw him as a man of profound beliefs, a man of integrity. When he heard their put-downs—for they talked on and on about his laziness—he merely muttered that he had no use for them. He was not gonna let anybody tell him what to do with his life.

Daddy Gus was a devout believer, a deacon at his church; he was one of the right-hand men of God. At church, everyone admired his calmness. Baba had no use for church. She liked nothing better than to tell us all the ways it was one big hypocritical place: "Why, I can find God anywhere I want to—I do not need a church." Indeed, when my grandmother died, her funeral could not take place in a church, for she had never belonged. Her refusal to attend church bothered some of her daughters, for they thought she was sinning against God, setting a bad example for the children. We were not supposed to listen when she began to damn the church and everybody in it.

Baba loved to "cuss." There was no bad word she was not willing to say. The improvisational manner in which she would string those words together was awesome. It was the goddamn sons of bitches who thought that they could fuck with her when they could just kiss her black ass. A woman of strong words and powerful metaphors, she could not read or write. She lived in the power of language. Her favorite sayings were a prelude for storytelling. It was she who told me, "Play with a puppy, he'll lick you in the mouth." When I heard this saying, I knew what was coming—a long polemic about not letting folks get too close, 'cause they will mess with you.

Baba loved to tell her stories. And I loved to hear them. She called me Glory. And in the midst of her storytelling she would pause to say, "Glory, are ya listenin'. Do you understand what I'm telling ya." Sometimes I would have to repeat the lessons I had learned. Sometimes I was not able to get it right and she would start again. When Mama felt I was learning too much craziness "over home" (that is what we called Baba's house), my visits were curtailed. As I moved into my teens I learned to keep to myself all the wisdom of the old ways I picked up over home.

Baba was an incredible quilt maker, but by the time I was old enough to really understand her work, to see its beauty, she was already having difficulty with her eyesight. She could not sew as much as in the old days, when her work was on everybody's bed. Unwilling to throw anything away, she loved to make crazy quilts, 'cause they allowed every scrap to be used. Although she would one day order patterns and make perfect quilts with colors that went together, she always collected scraps.

Long before I read Virginia Woolf's *A Room of One's Own* I learned from Baba that a woman needed her own space to work. She had a huge room for her quilting. Like every other space in the private world she created upstairs, it had her treasures, an endless array of hatboxes, feathers, and trunks filled with old clothes she had held on to. In room after room there were feather tick mattresses; when they were pulled back, the wooden slats of the bed were revealed, lined with exquisite hand-sewn quilts.

In all these trunks, in crevices and drawers were braided to-bacco leaves to keep away moths and other insects. A really hot summer could make cloth sweat, and stains from tobacco juice would end up on quilts no one had ever used. When I was a young child, a quilt my grandmother had made kept me warm, was my solace and comfort. Even though Mama protested when I dragged that old raggedy quilt from Kentucky to Stanford, I knew I needed that bit of the South, of Baba's world, to sustain me.

Like Daddy Gus, she was a woman of her word. She liked to declare with pride, "I mean what I say and I say what I mean." "Glory," she would tell me, "nobody is better than their word—if you can't keep ya word you ain't worth nothin' in this world." She would stop speaking to folk over the breaking of their word, over lies. Our mama was not given to loud speech or confronta-tion. I learned all those things from Baba—"to stand up and speak up" and not to "give a good goddamn" what folk who "ain't got a pot to pee in" think. My parents were concerned with their image in the world. It was pure blasphemy for Baba to teach that it did not matter what other folks thought—"Ya have to be right with yaself in ya own heart—that's all that mat-ters." Baba taught me to listen to my heart—to follow it. From her we learned as small children to remember our dreams in the night and to share them when we awakened. They would be in-terpreted by her. She taught us to listen to the knowledge in dreams. Mama would say this was all nonsense, but she too was known to ask the meaning of a dream.

In their own way my grandparents were rebels, deeply com-mitted to radical individualism. I learned how to be myself from them. Mama hated this. She thought it was important to be liked, to conform. She had hated growing up in such an eccentric, otherworldly household. This world where folks made their own wine, their own butter, their own soap; where chickens were raised, and huge gardens were grown for canning everything. This was the world Mama wanted to leave behind. She wanted store-bought things.

Baba lived in another time, a time when all things were produced in the individual household. Everything the family needed was made at home. She loved to tell me stories about learning to trap animals, to skin, to soak possum and coon in brine, to fry up a fresh rabbit. Though a total woman of the outdoors who could shoot and trap as good as any man, she still believed every woman should sew—she made her first quilt as a girl. In her world, women were as strong as men because they had to be. She had grown up in the country and knew that country ways were the best ways to live. Boasting about being able to do anything that a man could do and better, this woman who could not read or write was confident about her place in the universe.

My sense of aesthetics came from her. She taught me to really look at things, to see underneath the surface, to see the different shades of red in the peppers she had dried and hung in the kitchen sunlight. The beauty of the ordinary, the everyday, was her feast of light. While she had no use for the treasures in my granddaddy's world, he too taught me to look for the living spirit in things—the things that are cast away but still need to be touched and cared for. Picking up a found object he would tell me its story or tell me how he was planning to give it life again.

Connected in spirit but so far apart in the life of everydayness, Baba and Daddy Gus were rarely civil to each other. Every shared talk begun with goodwill ended in disagreement and contestation. Everyone knew Baba just loved to fuss. She liked a good war of words. And she was comfortable using words to sting and hurt, to punish. When words would not do the job, she could reach for the strap, a long piece of black leather that would leave tiny imprints on the flesh.

There was no violence in Daddy Gus. Mama shared that he had always been that way, a calm and gentle man, full of tenderness. I remember clinging to his tenderness when nothing I did was right in my mother's eyes, when I was constantly punished. Baba was not an ally. She advocated harsh punishment. She had no use for children who would not obey. She was never ever affectionate. When we entered her house, we gave her a kiss in greeting and that was it. With Daddy Gus we could cuddle, linger in his arms, give as many kisses as desired. His arms and heart were always open.

In the back of their house were fruit trees, chicken coops, and gardens, and in the front were flowers. Baba could make anything grow. And she knew all about herbs and roots. Her home remedies healed our childhood sicknesses. Of course she thought it crazy for anyone to go to a doctor when she could tell them just what they needed. All these things she had learned from her mother, Bell Blair Hooks, whose name I would choose as my pen name. Everyone agreed that I had the temperament of this great-grandmother I would not remember. She was a sharp-tongued woman. Or so they said. And it was believed I had inherited my way with words from her.

Families do that. They chart psychic genealogies that often overlook what is right before our eyes. I may have inherited my great-grandmother Bell Hook's way with words, but I learned to use those words listening to my grandmother. I learned to be courageous by seeing her act without fear. I learned to risk because she was daring. Home and family were her world. While my grandfather journeyed downtown, visited at other folks' houses, went to church, and conducted affairs in the world, Baba rarely left home. There was nothing in the world she needed. Things out there violated her spirit.

As a child I had no sense of what it would mean to live a life, spanning so many generations, unable to read or write. To me Baba was a woman of power. That she would have been extraordinarily powerless in a world beyond 1200 Broad Street was a thought that never entered my mind. I believed that she stayed home because it was the place she liked best. Just as Daddy Gus seemed to need to walk—to roam.

After his death it was easier to see the ways that they complemented and completed each other. For suddenly, without him as a silent backdrop, Baba's spirit was diminished. Something in her was forever lonely and could not find solace. When she died, tulips, her favorite flower, surrounded her. The preacher told us that her death was not an occasion for grief, for "it is hard to live in a world where your choicest friends are gone." Daddy Gus was the companion she missed most. His presence had always been the mirror of memory. Without it there was so much that could not be shared. There was no witness.

Seeing their life together, I learned that it was possible for women and men to fashion households arranged around their own needs. Power was shared. When there was an imbalance, Baba ruled the day. It seemed utterly alien to me to learn about black women and men not making families and homes together.

I had not been raised in a world of absent men. One day I knew I would fashion a life using the patterns I inherited from Baba and Daddy Gus. I keep treasures in my cigar box, which still smells after all these years. The quilt that covered me as a child remains, full of ink stains and faded colors. In my trunks are braided tobacco leaves, taken from over home. They keep evil away—keep bad spirits from crossing the threshold, like the ancestors they guard and protect.

GEOFFREY WOLFF

On the hot, breathless, soft, fragrant afternoon of my graduation from Princeton it seemed that everything good was not merely latent but unavoidable, folded and in the bag. I'd worked like a Turk those past years, and my labors had been rewarded and then some with fancy Latin on my fancy diploma, *summa* it said and summit I believed. Not one but two ex-girlfriends had come to the ceremony in front of lovely tree-shaded Nassau Hall, and so resolutely happy was I that it didn't even stain my pride to sweat through my shirt and gray worsted suit, to be capped like a monkey in tasseled mortarboard.

Each of my exes had brought me the same gift, a suitcase. It occurred to me that unarticulated longings were expressed by these mementos, and coming to them for visits wouldn't have answered their prayers. Sending me off solo on a long voyage

Geoffrey Wolff (to the left of the young gentleman wearing a tam-o'-shanter, a disdainful expression, and a bear's claw) and his Princeton suitemates, 1959.

would have been in the ballpark, Godspeed would have done their fantasies justice, *adiós* was more like it.

And that too was as I wished it! All was jake, a-okay, on the come and coming! Admitted, I had no money, but a job was waiting nigh September, far, far away, teaching in Turkey, which was even farther from my father in California than I was now in the Garden State, and the farther the better. The last time I had intersected with him, two years before, he had swept through Princeton in a car sought for repossession, charging clothes and books and jazz records to my accounts. My stepmother, having just left him again and for good, gave me unwelcome word of him a year later; he was in Redondo Beach, in trouble.

For me, that June, what was trouble? A college friend with a different kind of daddy, the kind who owned a fifty-foot paid-for ketch, had invited me to spend the summer with him on that boat in Massachusetts Bay, Buzzards Bay, Nantucket Sound, Vineyard Sound, Narragansett Bay. It was our onus to sail that *Sea Witch* from snug harbor to snug harbor, cleaning and polishing and varnishing, making the boat ready for his parents' pleasure if they wanted to come aboard, which they wouldn't because they had better places to play that summer, as though there could be a better place to play than where we were to be fed and paid to play. I was warned that sunburn was a lively danger, likewise hangovers from the free consumables at coming-out parties in Nonquitt and Nantucket, Newport and Edgartown. Dark and lonely work, but somebody had to do it.

Now, a few days after graduation, doing it, we were embarked. My suitcases and diploma were stored ashore with my passport and vaccination certificates and Greek tragedies in translation; we tugged at anchor off Cuttyhunk, drinking a rum drink to celebrate our third day at sea. There were four of us, two happy couples laughing and watching the sun fall, when my father got through on the radiotelephone. Writing about that conversation thirty-four years later I feel foggy dread, as though I've sailed on a cloudless day through deep clear water bang onto a reef. It's the nature of a radiotelephone conversation that everyone aboard can hear it, not to mention anyone else aboard any vessel within miles who wants to listen in.

This conversation mortified me. My dad stuttered flamboyantly. He did everything abundantly, elaborately, extravagantly, but his stuttering was grandiose. Moreover, he couldn't get the hang of the turn-and-turn-about of a radio conversation, in which one either speaks or listens. Listening was not my dad's thing, so I heard myself shouting at him, and worse, I heard myself stammering back, so that it must have seemed I was mocking the poor fellow, when in fact I was falling, as abruptly as a boat may fetch up on a shoal, into the speech defect I had inherited from him—nature or nurture, who cares?

While my friends, helplessly obliged to eavesdrop, pretended to have a conversation in the cockpit, I was below, where it was dark and close, as if the clean, salty air had been sucked from the cabin. I stretched the mike on its snaky cord as far from my friends as possible, but the loudspeaker stayed put, broadcasting his invitation:

My father wanted me to come to him for the summer, in La Jolla.

I said I wouldn't.

My father said he missed me.

I said nothing.

My father tried to tell me he had a j-j-j-job.

I said, really, how nice. (I thought, how novel, what a piquant notion, my dad working for a living.)

My father said congratulations on the degree.

I wondered how he'd guessed I had one.

He said congratulations on the job in Turkey, did I remember he'd lived there once upon a time?

I said I remembered.

He asked did I have a "popsie" aboard with me?

I reddened; it was quiet in the cockpit; I said I had to get off now, this was too expensive, far too complicated.

He said my brother was coming to La Jolla to visit from Washington state. Learned boy that I was, I didn't believe my father. I hadn't seen Toby for seven years.

My father said it again, Toby was right now on the road from Concrete, Washington, arriving in a couple of days.

I listened to static while gentle waves slapped the *Sea Witch*.

He said he'd send airfare.

I said sure. I thought fat chance.

I borrowed ticket money from the yachtsman dad and hopped a hound (more accurately a Trailway—cheaper) in New York. This would be the place to detail the squalor of a cross-country summer bus journey from the noxious flats of Jersey to the uncompromising wasteland of Death Valley—you know the drill, you've ridden a bus, you've read about the Joads. Assume I was sad, hungry, and as funky as everyone else aboard our land yacht, our prairie schooner. The one constant in addition to the diesely

whine while successive drivers went up through the gearbox—
do-re-mi-fa-sol-la-ti-do—and down—do-ti-la-sol . . . —was the
question I kept asking myself: *How had this happened to me? Why
was I here?*

You might think—noticing the books I was conspicuously
reading and annotating, and I'm afraid you were meant to notice
them and me—that the question *why was I here?* was a Big Question and that I was questing for a vision from Sophocles, Erich
Auerbach, Sartre, George Steiner. Boy oh boy, you think you
know your aliens! I felt so apart from my fellow passengers that I
believed I needed a visa to visit Earth. But at some point west of
Gila Bend and east of El Centro, with the air-conditioning on
the blink again, I commenced to reflect on the situation of La
Jolla—seaside, wasn't it? Even a martyr had to take time off for
a swim.

Hedonism, taking care of fun before taking care of business,
was a legacy from my father. For this he had been thrown out of
one boarding school after another, to the theatrical dismay of his
mother and father, a Hartford, Connecticut, surgeon. For this he
had also been thrown out of two colleges, neither of which, despite his testimony to the contrary, were fancy and ancient uni-
versities. For buying what he could not afford—sports cars and
sports coats, Patek-Philippe wristwatches, dinners at Mike Ro-
manoff's and 21, Leicas and Bolexes, Holland & Holland shot-
guns, whatever nice thing was around—he'd been fired from
jobs. These jobs as an airplane designer (I know, I know: he was
audacious) he had conned his way into with faked-up résumés.
Getting fired would put him in a bad mood, so he'd buy more
stuff; buying stuff intoxicated him, and so did booze. Drunk,
he'd turn on his first wife, my mother and Toby's. After fourteen

years of this, she told Dad to get lost, and I moved in with him. When I was seventeen, his second wife—her fortune and good mood seriously depressed by my old man—took a hike on him, and soon after that he took one on me. In the Wolff nuclear family, fission was all the rage.

Dad met me at the same bus station where he'd met Toby more than a week earlier. Visiting San Diego recently I was hard-pressed to find any site downtown as melodramatically seedy as my memory of that place, a garishly lit set dressed with tattoo parlors, bucket-of-blood bars, pawnshops, and, under the hard light of noon, my dad looking bewildered and lost. I had for many childhood years loved him recklessly, investing him with achievements and wisdom and powers beyond the reach of any mortal, and only a pinch less magnificent than the history and potential he had bestowed upon himself. Spare any father such impulsive love as I showered on that man. Later, when I became disillusioned, when I imagined that I understood Duke Wolff for what he really was—a deadbeat bullshit artist with a veneer of charm rubbed right through from negligent over-exercise— I hated him, and like the love before it, that hate too was indulgent, exorbitant.

This June afternoon outside the bus depot, examining my father blinking behind the thick lenses of owlish Goldwater specs, I was too wary to indulge contempt. The eyeglasses, out of register with Duke's formerly stylish presentations, were the least of it. Even at his lowest he'd enjoyed flamboyant tempera-mental resources: flash and spritz and nonchalance. Now he seemed timid, dulled, hungover. No: that wasn't it either; I was all too inured to his hangovers, which used to provoke in my dad a manic snap, as though he'd decided that if this was as bad as it got, bring it on, let's start another IV Mount Gay rum drip. What I was seeing lumbering toward me was a crummy linenish jacket. This wasn't what I'd have expected: seersucker, maybe, or the soiled white linen suit that Sydney Greenstreet might sport—tits-up in the tropics and all that—but not this, some thing on whose behalf a thousand polyesters had lost their lives, some rag that needed a cleaning the day it was sold, tarted up with cheapjack brass crested buttons. From Duke's good old bad old days of smart tailoring, what a fall was here! Halting toward me was a zombie. Dad Wolff looked as though he'd been shot smack in the heart with about 500 cc of Thorazine. Talk about taking the edge off! He looked like they'd sawed through his brain.

My brother, Toby, fifteen, was with him, hanging back gingerly, vigilant. I felt like someone to whom something bad would soon happen; Toby looked like someone to whom it had already happened. This was the more alarming because he looked so wakeful and sharp. He had a strong, bony face, with steady eyes and a jutting chin. He was tall and lean, handsome, like our mother. He didn't appear vulnerable; he gave an impression of competence, but after all, he was a kid.

I hadn't seen Toby during the past seven years, but we'd recently been in touch by telephone and letter, and I knew that he'd had a rocky time of it with his stepfather. Coming across the country to see my only sibling, I'd phoned from a roadside diner to tell Duke which bus to meet and I'd reached Toby. He didn't know where our father had disappeared to. No sooner had Toby arrived than Dad had taken off with a woman friend in a fancy

Italian car. He had left his teenaged son with a hotel phone number and a vague assurance that he'd return to La Jolla in a few days.

Behind the wheel of the hubby-mummy rented Pontiac, driving to La Jolla, Duke was stiff and tentative. This was unlike him. I remembered him as a bold driver, fast and cocksure, every little journey to the grocery store a high-octane adventure in squealing tires and red-lined rpms. Now Dad held to the slow lane, glancing anxiously in the rearview. His face had once been imposing, Mussolini-monumental; now his nose was bulbous, stippled with burst blood vessels. The few times he spoke, I saw that his false teeth, what he used to call China clippers, were loose against his gums. I had questions: Where had he gone, leaving Toby alone? How could he take time off from his job? Asking this question I gave the impression, meant to give it, that I didn't believe he had a job. How soon could he give me cash (I came down hard on *cash,* to distinguish it from a check or an IOU) to repay my yachtsman classmate's yachtsman daddy? These questions immediately returned us to our fundamental relationship: I was the hectoring (and mind-dullingly dull) parent; Duke was the irresponsible (and charmingly fun-loving) kid. The exchange didn't leave much for Toby to do, except sit in the backseat and study his fingers, as though he might be looking hard at his hole cards.

Duke was miserly with basic information—what exactly he did for a living, where he had gone "in the desert" (as he put it) or why. But as we approached La Jolla he became effusive about his "lady friend." This conversation had the effect of making Toby visibly uncomfortable, inasmuch as it had been my father's

stated ambition, made explicit to Toby, to re-up with our mom
if everything this summer went swimmingly, as of course it had
to. This nutty scheme had (no, wonders never do cease) a certain appeal to my mother, who has had a lifelong weakness for
nutty schemes. Her marriage to her second husband, like her
marriage to Duke before that, was a disaster, and Duke after all
did live in southern California, and my mom, freezing up near
the Canadian border, had always had, as she put it, "sand between my toes." But even this quixotic woman—who had decided a few years earlier that it was a sage idea to drive from
Florida to Utah to explore for uranium without knowing what
uranium was or why anyone wanted it—was on hold as far as a
reenrollment in Dad's program was concerned, waiting to get a
report card from Toby on Duke's attendance and comportment.

When we rolled up in front of a tiny bungalow east of Girard Avenue, my befuddlement increased. The woman who
greeted us, as warily as Toby and I greeted her, was nothing like
my father's type. He was drawn to palefaces, to blue eyes, to un-
derstated clothes. This woman was sunburnt brown, her leathery skin set off with much jangly jewelry. She wore many, many
rings of the turquoise family, accessorizing showy peasant duds
from south of the border, busy with appliqué and bold stitch-
ing. She wore, for God's sake, cowgirl boots ornamented with
horsehair.

We stood beside the car shaking her ringed hand and listening to her bracelets ring like chimes; we admired her cactus garden; she got to listen to my father—and not, I suspected, for the
first time—inflate my achievements at college and Toby's in high
school; she didn't invite Toby or me inside. She didn't invite Dad
inside either, but it was clear that inside was where he was going,
and without his only children. He gave us rudimentary instruc-

tions to "my flat near the beach." Toby, manifestly eager to get away from where we were, assured me he knew the way. Duke said he'd be along soon, he'd bring home a nice supper. I asked how he'd get home from there, and he waved vaguely, mumbled "taxi." His lady friend seemed as unhappy as a person can be without flooding the earth with tears. Duke, by contrast, had abruptly come awake to joy; he was peppy, full of beans.

"Don't you two rascals go getting in t-t-t-trouble," he warned. "And if the manager badgers you about the rent, tell him to go f-f-f-f . . ."

"Go f-f-fish," I s-s-s-said.

Driving south through the attractive neighborhoods to our little second-floor studio apartment on Playa del Sur, fifty yards from the beach, I was mostly preoccupied with Toby, glad for the chance to be alone with him. He too relaxed, lit a Lucky Strike expertly with his lighter, inhaled intemperately, remarked that it had been an oddball visit so far. I asked him to steer while I lit a Camel expertly with my lighter, inhaled intemperately, and warned him that smoking was bad for his wind, especially if he planned to make a name for himself playing football at the Hill School back in Pennsylvania, where he was beginning on full scholarship in September.

My avuncular manner surprised me. I prided myself on being a laissez-faire kind of guy, I'll look out for me, you look out for you. Maybe I was practicing to become a teacher. Maybe I was out of my depth.

I unpacked my worldly goods—mostly books, a few jazz LPs (Bessie Smith, Bud Powell, the Miles Davis quintet, with Coltrane) I carried with me everywhere—and Toby wanted to show me the beach. This generosity was all Wolff—sharing the good news, keeping alert to fun. By then it was late afternoon, and I worried that Dad might come home to an empty apartment, but Toby argued soberly that he didn't imagine Duke would be rushing home from his friend's house. I saw the wisdom in this hunch.

And so, dressed in long trousers and boat shoes and a white Lacoste tennis shirt, I accompanied Toby across Vista del Mar and Neptune Place to the Pump House, and down concrete steps to the beach. The first things I noticed were not the bitchin' sets of waves breaking way offshore, nor the surfers paddling way out there waiting to ride, nor the surfers with lots of white hair waxing their boards near the water's edge. I noticed, of course, the babes, and so did Toby.

"Hubba hubba," he said with reassuring irony, a family vice.

So we sat for a long time on a couple of hand towels, talking about the future, with our eyes cocked on the very here and now, avoiding the subject of our father. Toby was witty, resourceful, a hit parade of corny songs, which he was willing to sing out loud: "On the Wings of a Dove" and "Calendar Girl." He could do Chuck Berry's "Sweet Little Sixteen" and Hank Williams—"Hey, hey good-lookin', whatcha got cookin', howsabout cookin' something up with me?" He could do a Jimmy Rogers yodel in caricature of a locomotive whistle, and he knew the gospel classics, "The Old Rugged Cross." He did tenor lead, I did baritone. Even then, he remembered the words I'd forgot. The dynamite chicks stared frankly at us and our noise, with what I imagined that afternoon—but never imagined again—was interest.

· · ·

It didn't get dark till nine or so. We waited. The landlord came asking for rent. He was kind, patient, pretended to believe that we didn't know where our old man could be found. He said it had gone on too long now, that Duke was months behind, that he had no choice . . .

"Do what you have to do," I said, thinking about a sailboat waiting for me back East.

"Such a shame," he said and sighed, "a man of his attainments, with his education!"

"Uh-huh," I said.

When the landlord left, Toby said, "Tell me something. Did Dad really go to Yale?"

"What do you think?"

"So that would pretty much rule out his graduate degree from the Sorbonne?"

We laughed together, bless us.

Sometime after midnight we quit talking, stopped listening to my jazz records and Dad's Django Reinhardt and Joe Venuti. We'd eaten a couple of cans of Dinty Moore stew, knocked back some Canadian Club we'd found on a high shelf of the mostly bare cupboard. We'd each asked aloud where the other thought Duke might be. We'd wondered aloud whether we should look for him, but I was sure he was drunk, and he had always been a mean drunk, and I didn't want to find him. I didn't trust myself to keep my hands to myself while he sat on the edge of his bed in his boxers, snarling about how ungrateful I was, how grievously I had kicked him in the ass when he was down: *You're a real piece of work, aren't you?* I'd heard it; I didn't think I could hear it again, especially if it came to be Toby's turn.

A couple of hours before dawn his lady friend phoned. She was hysterical, said she didn't know what to do, he wouldn't leave, wouldn't move, wouldn't speak. He'd rock back and forth weeping.

"You've got to get him out of here. I can't take this. What if my husband comes snooping around?"

So I phoned the police. By the time Toby and I got there, the police had called for an ambulance. Dad was breathing, but save for the technicality of being alive, he was gone from this world. His lady friend too said, as so many ex-bosses, ex-friends, ex-wives, creditors, teachers, doctors, parole officers before and after had said, *A man with his educational attainments, what a pity!*

They checked him into Scripps Memorial Hospital. The police had investigated his wallet and he had Blue Cross. Now *this* was a shock, because he had Blue Cross owing to the fact that he also had a job! Just as he'd said. He worked for General Dynamics Astronautics. By sunup I knew this, and knew as well that he was catatonic, and roughly what catatonia was. He would be removed that afternoon to a "more appropriate facility," and I could guess what that would be. As obdurately as my heart had hardened, I heard myself telling the doctor to tell Dad his sons were here for him, we were behind him all the way. Toby nodded.

"Well," the doctor said, "he has said a few words. He keeps asking for a woman who lives in town. Could you help out with this, maybe let her know he wants to see her?"

"No," I said.

That morning I worked out a deal with the landlord. On principle he wouldn't let us stay in the apartment on which so much rent was due, but he'd let me lease, in my name, an identical unit down the exterior hall, same monthly rent but this time he required an up-front security deposit, first and last month in cash or by cashier's check by the end of business tomorrow.

I borrowed it from a classmate, the roommate of the son of the yachtsman dad from whom I'd borrowed my bus fare. Tangled, wot? It took a boy of my educational attainments to keep all those debts straight, all the lines of credit, but a boy of my educational attainments also knew how to cash in on sympathy. My classmate friend cabled the money from New York that afternoon, and that night Toby and I moved our father's entirely unpaid-for worldly goods to our new residence.

Drunk on resourcefulness, I bought a car and found a job the very next day. The car caught my eye on the lot of Balboa Auto Sales. I'm confident of the name of the dealer because I still have a copy of my stiff reply from Istanbul to a bill collector in San Diego (Hi there, Mr. Ben D. Warren!) begging for the final $150 of the $300 purchase price on a '52 Ford convertible, cream, with torn red vinyl upholstery and bald whitewall tires and an appetite for oil that gave my jaunty wreck a range of about three miles between lube-stops, which made the drive to Tijuana, a popular excursion in the coming weeks, a hardship that only the señoritas of the rowdier cantinas could ameliorate. Ask Toby: he was in charge of oil changing, while I was in charge of drinking and whoring.

The job was easier to cop than the automobile. I simply went to Dad's employer, on the theory that they needed to replace him, and offered my services. A few weeks before in Princeton, getting my diploma, I'd suspected life was going to go smoothly for me, but this . . . *this* was silky! To build rockets during the age of the putative missile gap, the government had contracted with General Dynamics Astronautics to supply Atlas ICBMs at cost-plus. Now cost-plus, I don't have to tell you, is one sweet deal. The greater the cost, the greater the plus, so personnel basically threw money at me when I walked through its door with a bachelor's degree in English Literature. Every time I opened my mouth to mention courses I'd taken—history, American civilization, Spanish—they tossed in another jackpot, so that by day's end I was an engineering writer for more than eight hundred a month, with an advance from the credit union and a complete understanding of how my father had found a job with these cheerful jokers. Don't you miss the Cold War!

Dad was embalmed in an academy of laughter down in Chula Vista, not much of a detour from my weekend line of march to Tijuana. Toby and I were permitted to visit only on Saturdays, which suited my schedule fine, and when we visited he behaved like his old self, which, on the best day of his life, did not display a mastery of your everyday parenting skills. He seemed oblivious to any inconvenience he might have caused his sons, made no mention of the carnage of Toby's first week in La Jolla. Quotidian challenges were beneath his notice: whether he'd lost his job (he had), how much longer his insurance would support his treatment (not long enough), by what transport we'd conveyed ourselves to our audience with him (he did fret about a car "I had to desert in the desert," a play on words that amused him so exceedingly that he neglected the situation's starker implication, soon enough to weigh heavily on him).

We met a few of his new friends, men and women jollier than I would have expected, but their serenity might have been an outcome of the electric shock therapy Duke resolutely and justly resisted. He was busy with workshop therapy, making a leather portfolio into which he burned my initials. This was a difficult gift to receive, and to hold now.

Not least because it fell into a category of assets—personal-ized keepsakes—that opened a painful fissure between Toby and me. One thing, and it was a *thing,* was uppermost on my father's mind when my brother and I visited his asylum in Chula Vista. This was a silver cigarette lighter inscribed to him in London after the blitz by friends in the RAF when he was in England on behalf of North America to deliver P-51 Mustangs. He wanted that lighter; jeepers, did he *desire* that silver lighter; did we grasp that the lighter MATTERED to him? He decided that we had lost it during our move from one apartment to another. Oh, was he disappointed! His new friends would like to see that inscribed silver lighter, and he'd like to show it to them. Why didn't we just run back to La Jolla and find it, "chop-chop"?

It's amazing what kids—even kids as old as I was then, old enough to buy a car on the installment plan and to sign a lease—will accept as the way of the world. I don't mean merely that kids are subject to arbitrary tyrannies, though they are; I mean that until I had sons I never really understood how emotionally derelict my father was. I judged the cost of his selfishness on an empirical scale, by the measurable havoc he inflicted on me. It wasn't till I had sons that I began to understand that such lunatic solipsism as Duke's shook the rudiments of his sons' worlds, mis-aligned the paths connecting us, upset proportion, priority, ratio, reason itself.

How else explain us searching together the fifty-foot walk-way connecting those two apartments, as well as the shrubs below that walkway, as well as our new apartment? What warped sense of duty provoked us to knock on the door of the new tenants' apartment during the dinner hour to persuade them that we needed to search every inch of their abode for a lost cigarette lighter? And failing to find it, to phone the car rental company, the very company that was seeking payment from our father, to ask if a silver cigarette lighter had been found in one of their Pontiacs?

I think now, considering my own dear sons, beginning at last to fathom how difficult it is to be anyone's son, that our father drove us insane that summer. I'll speak for myself: he pushed me to the edge and over it.

My life with Toby seemed on the surface, subtracting weekend visits to the loony bin in Chula Vista and the brothels of Tijuana, workaday. After staring at my pencils and at my colleagues staring at their pencils for six of the eight hours I "worked" in a hangar, the Ford would stumble up the coast to La Jolla, trailing cloud banks of exhaust, a whole weather system. I drove with the torn top up to shelter myself from the black fog that swirled around me when I was stopped in traffic.

But there I go, looking at the dark side, getting gothic on you. At day's end there was home, simple but clean. And the beach. Ah, Windansea! Remember my first visit there, my eyes as big as plates, those surfer chicks, what Dad called popsies? Well, I hadn't completed my second walk from the Pump House south toward Big Rock Reef when a teen approached me.

"Hey!" she said. Her toenails were painted vivid red. Her hair was . . . guess what color. She was . . . (Did you guess pretty?)

I cradled my paperback. "Hey, yourself," I came back.

"You from around here?" she asked.

I chuckled. "No. No, not at all, just visiting on my way to Istanbul."

"Is that on the beach?" (No, of course she didn't ask that. There's no call to get snotty here, just because I was about to have my heart broken.) "Huh?" (*That's* what she said.)

"Are you from around here?" was my trenchant rejoinder.

She was, she said, she was. And her business with me was to invite me to a keg party that night down in Pacific Beach. She was glad I could make it. We'd have a lot of fun. Was I sure I had the address written down? She checked what I'd written on the title page of Camus's *The Stranger.*

"Thing is, me and my friends need some cash to front the keg."

Thing was, I didn't have any cash in my bathing suit. Could I bring it when I came? No? Okay, hang on, don't go anywhere, I'll just run home and get it, which I did. She was waiting by a VW van, pretty much holding her pretty hand out.

I don't have to tell you how the party went. What party, eh? What Surf Boulevard in Pacific Beach?

Seven years later, reading Tom Wolfe's title essay in *The Pump House Gang,* I felt a full flush of shame rise from my toes. The keg scam was a chestnut among the surfers and surfer-babes at Windansea. But that was the least of my mortification there. Frank laughter was the worst of it. Back home at the Jersey shore or on the beach at Watch Hill, blinking contemplatively behind my groundbreaking round, silver-framed glasses (so far ahead of the curve that the nickname "granny glasses" hadn't yet been invented), in my navy polo shirt to hide my chubby tits, in my Brooks Brothers madras bathing costume, by George I was a stud muffin! Here, carrying a Great Book past those hep long-boarders in their nut-hugger nylon suits with competition stripes, I was a freaking joke!

So where, during these humiliating hours after work, was Toby? Safe inside, at his books, writing essays I assigned him. It took him a while to forgive me for practicing my apprentice teaching skills on him. To prepare him for the exactions of a classical education at the Hill School, I obliged him to do a day's work while I did a day's work, to read a book a day and write an essay every week: "Blindness and Insight in *King Lear* and the *Oedipus Tyrannus*"; "The Boundaries of Sea and River: Liberty and Bondage in *Moby Dick* and *Huckleberry Finn*." I guess what I knew best came in pairs. It was crazy the hoops I made my beleaguered, injured, perplexed little brother jump through. He wrote them; he was a better reader and writer for them. But I was a tin-pot despot, as arbitrary in my edicts as Duke sending us on a treasure hunt for his fire-stick. No wonder Toby stole from his father and lied to me.

Did you guess he'd had the sacred lighter all along? Used it to spark up that Lucky during our ride in the Pontiac from the leathery, jangly lady's bungalow to Dad's sea-near studio apartment.

He slept on a pull-out sofa bed in our one-roomer, and mid-August, when the alarm clock woke me for work, I saw the stupid, pretty thing on the floor beneath his blue jeans. In the sullen light of dawn, I made out an inscription engraved on it. My father's initials in elegant sans serif. No RAF boys, of course, but another name for sure, a new engraving, commissioned up on Girard Avenue, TOBY. I remembered the hours we'd spent together hunting for that costly goddamned thing, Toby's helpful suggestions where next to search: the beach, Dad's suit pockets, maybe it had fallen out of Dad's trouser pocket into one of the shoes in his closet?

That morning was awful, and I want to pull a curtain across it. Duke was coming "home" from Chula Vista that afternoon; I was meant to pick him up after work. I didn't know what we'd all do, where we'd live, how we'd sit together in a room, how we'd look at one another, what in the world we were supposed to do now. What I knew for sure: Toby hated us both, his father and his brother. I knew why he hated the one, but not the other. Now I think I know all I'll ever know about that aspect of that summer, and all I want to say to Toby is, Forgive me. Even though he has pardoned me, and himself, just this last time, Forgive me.

I fetched Duke; he raged at Toby. We sent my brother home to my mother on a bus. As bad as it was between my father and me, after Toby left it got worse. My father wasn't allowed to drink—all that medication—but of course he drank. How many days did the nightmare last? Few, I think. He tried to talk me into staying with him instead of going to Turkey. I managed not to laugh in his face. My work at Astro was a mercy, got me out of the apartment. My infamy on the beach was a joy, got me away from him. And I'd invited a couple of visitors, Princeton friends. One was coming up from Mexico in a Cadillac hearse, the other, from whom I'd borrowed the money to rent our apartment, was in the navy, coming to San Diego to join his aircraft carrier. I'd paid him back; breaking a Wolff family tradition, I'd repaid all my debts to friends that summer.

While my erstwhile classmate with the hearse was visiting,

Duke was arrested in San Diego. For a wonder, he wasn't drunk and he wasn't up to mischief. He was buying breakfast food at a late-hours store and he'd made a U-turn in my Ford. He'd stuttered when the policeman stopped him. They took him downtown. It went hard on him. By the time my friend and I arrived in the hearse, they were ready to let him go. This was the old police station, gone now, surrendered to gentrification down near Seaport Village. Back then it had a holding tank, and my father was in it, stone terrified. Before they let him go they checked with Sacramento. They got back a complicated story. It went very hard on him, grand theft auto for the Abarth-Allemagne roadster in the desert, burned and sand-blasted by a desert storm. My father wanted me to go bail for him, but he wouldn't promise to show up in court, or even to stay in California.

I didn't go bail; I went to Istanbul.

Then was then. I try to explain to my wife, to my sons. They try to understand, and they've done a good job of it. The only way I know how to explain is on the page. It's a bitch getting the tone right. Now, writing this, I feel jumpy again after many years of feeling a warm embrace of resignation. That's okay. These shifts aren't spurious, I believe. Family stories are always fluid, and to be emotionally exact is to be inconsistent. Toby and I have talked a lot about this. We've talked a lot about a lot. We talk all the time, and as good as a friendship can get, that's how good I think ours is. When I told him I'd found the apartment where we spent the summer of '61, he seemed interested enough, but not *too* interested. When I told him I'd taken snapshots of the apartment, he didn't ask for copies.

He lifted a trinket that summer, my father lifted a car. Stealing: Jesus, Princeton had an honor code, it seemed like a really big deal, where could stealing lead? Where did it send my dad? That pal who loaned me money? The one I'd invited to visit just about the time my dad disappeared into the system and I fled to Asia Minor? He stole my dad's best shoes. He told me this in an expensive automobile driving to a fancy dinner party at a gentlemen's club on Society Hill in Philadelphia. We were purring along in his Mercedes, snug in our navy blue topcoats and leather gloves and cashmere scarves. It was snowing. I had mentioned a few hours earlier to my old chum that I'd been back in La Jolla after all these years, back to the apartment at Playa del Sur. He'd seemed uncomfortable to hear this, and I understood his discomfort to stem from the disgrace visited on my family name that summer.

"I've been in that apartment," my friend said.

"I don't think so," I said. "You were supposed to visit me there, but then Dad went to jail and I went to . . ."

". . . to Istanbul," my amigo finished. "No, I've been there."

"I don't believe . . ."

"Hush," he said. "Let me tell you."

We were purring along the Schuylkill River now, and the headlights from cars on the expressway dimly lit the black water. Big wet flakes flew at our windshield; the dash glowed greenly. The car was heavy and solid; we were heavy and solid. My friend had been successful in business, investing prudently but shrewdly the inheritances of people who trusted his judgment and honor. His voice was measured. He told me. He told me how he had got the landlord at Playa del Sur, who didn't yet know I'd run out on him just after running out on my father, to let him in. How he had waited there. How he had had a beer or two from the fridge, and then a glass or two or three of the Wild Turkey

I was drinking back then. How he had listened to the record player. How he had stretched out and taken a nap. How he had wanted to walk down to the beach, but the landlord wouldn't give him a key. How he had waited and waited for me to come back from work. How he began to feel pissed off, put-upon. How he couldn't wait any longer; the *Saratoga* was cruising west; he was due aboard. How he had noticed my dad's shoes in the closet, really nice shoes, beautifully cared for, Church shoes, dark brown cap-toes. How something—boredom?—had urged him to try those shoes on his own feet. How they had fit as though they were made for him. How he had stolen them.

"And there was a jacket, too. Nice tweed job. I don't think it was your jacket. I didn't recognize it from college."

"What color?" I wanted to know.

"Greenish, heather, I guess you'd call it. Nubby but *soft,* a really nice tweed sport coat."

"It wouldn't have been mine," I said. "I didn't own a jacket that fits that description," I lied.

"How about that," my old friend said.

"What the hell," I said, "that was a long time ago."

You see, in Philadelphia, so far from Windansea that winter night, at last, I was finished with all this, who stole what from whom, who borrowed and who paid, who was owed what. I'm finally at the end of all that. This time I mean it. This time, again, I really mean it.

STUART DYBEK

T he shadow of a hawk swooped over the earth, but there wasn't a hawk in the sky. It was Toczi Groszek, who, dressed in his dark cloak, was more shadow than bird.

When the Krasnoludki saw the shadow they hid under mushrooms.

But it was already too late. Toczi Groszek had spotted the glint of the gold they had disguised as honey in a tree of bees.

Wearing an undertaker's suit that made him appear to be a grackle, Toczi Groszek hopped through the forest, leading Wali Gora to the hiding place. Wali Gora held a sack to the entrance of the hive and filled it with bees, then filled a second sack with gold.

From a distance the hum of bees in the sack sounded like violins, and the jangle of gold like a tambourine to Wirwy Dump, a giant who had been spading up a river. He came running, knocking trees out of the way with his enormous spade and hollering, "Hey, Gypsies! Everything in these woods is mine!" He knocked Wali Gora down with his spade

Stuart Dybek with
his grandfather and grandmother

and buried him in a deep grave, then greedily opened up one of the sacks, but it was the sack of angry bees, and Wiruy Dump ran off through the forest trailing bees behind him like a comet's tail.

Toczi Groszek took the gold to a crossroads and traded it to passing beggars for their ragged clothes.

Deep under the earth, Wali Gora was eating potatoes and growing bigger and bigger. One day in spring, Wali Gora would grow up out of the earth. At first, he would think he was a tree, and birds would build nests in his hair and bees store honey in his throat. But then, when autumn would come and all the trees would stand naked without their leaves, Wali Gora would understand his mistake and sadly realize he was still a man.

But until that happened—until Wali Gora would rise again out of the earth—Toczi Groszek put on the beggars' rags each evening at dusk and became a flock of pigeons that rose into the sky as if returning home. The pigeons circled Wali Gora's grave, and settling down upon it, they tucked their heads under their wings.

Shortly after he'd come over on the boat from Poland, my grandfather was buried alive for two days during a mine disaster in Johnstown, Pennsylvania. I remember being told that what was worse even than the pain of his pinned leg or the total darkness and the bone-chilling damp, worse than the thirst and fear and the helpless waiting were the sounds of the miners trapped around him, crushed and groaning in their final agonies, crying for help and praying in languages he didn't understand. My grandfather and a mule were the only survivors. Later in life, when my grandmother would complain about his odd, intractable ways, she'd always say, "That's something that only Pa and the stubborn mule would understand." When the rescue team finally dug him out he was singing at the top of his lungs in Polish, as he had the entire two days in order to drown out the sound of the suffering around him. He hadn't realized the other miners had gone silent. They said it was a miracle that he'd survived, but he ascribed his survival to the fifth of vodka he'd snuck down with him past Mahoney, the tough Irish foreman, and claimed that the only miracle was that the bottle hadn't broken.

He was still stubbornly surviving on vodka when I knew him, which was only for the first six years of my life, and still singing drunkenly in Polish. His name for me was Stulush. I was his firstborn grandson, and my many aunts and uncles, his children, had taken to calling me The Great Stulush. I didn't refer to him as my grandfather, but as my Dzia-dzia, which is pronounced as if it is spelled *jah-jah*. It means grandfather in Polish, and yet a Dzia-dzia seemed to me something other than simply a grandfather, something more and something less. It was a word that conveyed both presence and absence, that described someone who was at once central and peripheral to a family, someone near who had remained from far away, someone ancient, older than America. A Dzia-dzia was a paradox, a mystery.

He didn't speak much English, and I didn't understand Polish beyond the rudimentary words—although I thought I actually *was* speaking Polish when we conversed in an immigrant's tongue of broken English in which *shoes* were *shoeza* or *booteh,* and *money* was *dollarda,* and *car* was *cara.* By logical extension it seemed to me that *socks* would be *socksa* and *gloves* would be *glovsa,* and that speaking Polish was easy once one got the knack.

However it was that we managed to communicate, I knew

that he was a great teller of stories. After his wake, when the family gathered at Bishop's Chili, what they recalled about him besides his drinking and his brutal temper was his stories. Their most forgiving memories seemed to be of the times when they were children and he would gather them around the coal stove on winter nights. Dressed in his *zimowe gaczie*—his winter underwear, he'd tell them about the bewitched pigeons that were actually nobles who had been transformed centuries ago and still roosted in Saint Mary's Church in the center of Kraków, hooting at dawn and dusk like haunted souls. He'd tell about the *Krasnoludki*—fairies dressed in red—and of Wali Gora, whose name means Tear Down Mountains, and of a giant named Wirwy Dump, whose name means Tear Up Oaks, and a strange wanderer who could change shapes, named Toczi Groszek.

He told the same stories to me on summer afternoons when my mother and I would visit the two-story white frame house where she'd grown up on Seventeenth Street. The house faced the railroad tracks and the enormous concrete grain elevator of the J. J. Badenoch Company that rose over the southwest side of Chicago in a way that I imagined the Great Pyramid towered above Egypt. He'd summon me up to the bare, baking attic where he kept a pigeon loft. The room always resonated with a haunting sound as if someone was blowing air over the lip of an empty bottle. From the attic, we'd climb a homemade ladder through a trapdoor onto the roof and sit at the edge of the trapdoor with our legs dangling down into the attic while above us stretched a dizzying blue sky. Sometimes, keeping a hold on one of my trouser legs, he'd let me stand on the roof; I liked to peer down into the backyard, where my grandmother kept chickens in a chickenwire pen. Inside the pen was the stump of a chopping block for whacking off their heads. It bothered me that the block was in plain view of the chickens; I didn't think they needed to be reminded of it.

Dzia-dzia's pigeons weren't for eating. They were racing pigeons. When he was still back in the Old Country, he'd been drafted into the Austrian army, and it had been his job to tend a loft of messenger pigeons. I'd heard from my mother how, when she was a girl, Dzia-dzia would pack his pigeons into a car on Saturdays and drive a hundred miles to Indiana for competitions in which men released their homing pigeons to see which ones made it back and which of those birds were the fastest. I'd watch the gentleness with which he held his white birds in his tough, gnarled hands. He'd let me stroke their feathers before he'd toss them into flight, and we'd watch as they circled above the house and then flew higher, toward the grain elevator, where I'd lose sight of them in the whirl of birds that constantly circled J. J. Badenoch's. But Dzia-dzia could track his pigeons even in a flock—he'd point when they finally flew off on their own, out of the neighborhood, over the city to deliver whatever secret message he had whispered before releasing them into the sky.

While we waited for the pigeons to return, he would tell me stories. Mostly all I remember is vivid fragments like snatches of dreams, but perhaps that's how they were told to me in the first place. In one story Wali Gora, Wirwy Dump, and Toczi Groszek joined forces to fight for some damsel against a creature that was part dragon and part eagle, a creature so powerful that it buried Wali Gora and Wirwy Dump up to their eyes. But Toczi Groszek bargained to free them and to save the damsel by feeding the dragon-eagle one of his arms.

They were fierce stories that he acted out, gnawing at his own arm, making it disappear down his shirt, so that his sleeve flapped empty as an amputee's. His hazel eyes would flash like an eagle's and his nose would thrust forward as if it were a beak. His receding hair was a dirty gray blond, and he had wild, unkempt eyebrows that my uncles referred to as handlebar brows and that looked to me like wings about to fly off with his face. The hands that he formed into talons were hardened as if the skin had calcified, and were lined with what could have been veins of coal.

On our walks down Eighteenth Street, he used to entertain me by holding firecrackers. I'd touch the glowing tip of his stubby cigarette to the wicks of the firecrackers and jump back while they exploded between his fingers. It frightened me. Afterwards he'd laugh uproariously and show me his hand blackened and smelling of gunpowder, but still intact, and then taking my hand in his, he'd limp along to the next tavern. Sometimes he'd sing Polish songs as we walked down the street—a song that went *hupi shupi, hupi shupi,* and a song called *"Krakowiaczek ci ja,"* which meant "I'm a little boy from Kraków." When he sang it I'd wonder if it was one of the songs he'd sung while trapped in the mine. His voice was gravelly but still strong, a strength he ascribed to his enormous Adam's apple. He was proud of my voice, which was deep for my age, and he would lift me up and stand me on top of the bar and have me sing. "Ol' Man River" was my specialty. The men in the bar would applaud and Dzia-dzia would hoist me down carefully, as if he were handling a pigeon or packing up a valuable musical instrument. They'd set me up with a stein of root beer, and afterwards Dzia-dzia and I would head down Hoyne Avenue to the next joint, for more singing and more root beer for me and boilermakers for him. At some point, we'd end up standing in an alley, peeing side by side in broad daylight as I'd been taught never to do.

When after a series of strokes he was confined to the

Chicago State Hospital—a mental hospital that had a wing for stroke victims—he somehow managed to sneak a bottle of vodka in there with him, too, and he died in the middle of the night just before my aunt Hana's wedding day.

It seemed to me that instead of feeling grief, everyone else in the family was simply annoyed with him for being so stubborn as to keep drinking just when Hana, his lovely youngest daughter, was about to be married. They went on with the wedding without him—in spite of him—as if he had died as he had lived, in spite of them.

It's obvious to me now what emotional compromises to go on with the wedding, with their lives, must have been required for my mother and my aunts and uncles—his eight children— who'd grown up with his drinking and brawling and disappearances and his temper. But when he died, I was far too young to understand any of that. How would I have known that he treated his grandchild with a gentleness that his own children had not experienced?

Aunt Hana, my favorite aunt, had been my baby-sitter since I was born. She looked like a movie star in her bridal gown. She married my uncle Tony, whom my Dziz-dzia had referred to as Tony Baloney. He'd had nicknames for her other boyfriends, too. There was Sherman the German and Phillip the Tylek— *tylek* being a word for butt, frequently applied to the part of the chicken that was thrown to the cat. Her boyfriends usually avoided coming over to the house on Seventeenth, except for Tony, an ex-marine who'd fought on Iwo Jima. He was a great guy, who took me to Cubs' games and to drive-in movies with him and Aunt Hana. At the big reception after the wedding, Tony joked to me, "Busy time, huh, kid? Wedding and funeral in the same week. Well, that's life in a nutshell."

"Tony," Aunt Hana said, punching him in the arm, "what are you telling him?"

They had the reception in the VFW hall. There was a white cake that looked like a miniature temple. I was sure that the bride and groom perched at its pinnacle were exact replicas of Aunt Hana and Uncle Tony. There was a brassy polka band, and the musicians all wore cellophane hats and blew noisemakers as if it were New Year's Eve. I danced whirling across the floor with Aunt Hana and several of her bridesmaids, and Tony gave me sips of the melted ice at the bottom of his highball glasses. There was a long table covered with white paper and bowls of snacks: chips, pretzels, stacks of rye bread, kielbasa ringed around bowls of horseradish, platters of kolacky, and oranges stuck with toothpicks that looked like the spiked heads of maces. Empty longnecks of beer and half-drunk highball glasses accumulated amidst the snacks, and at some point my uncle Caz, who'd been whooping like a maniac on the dance floor, hoisted me up on the table and yelled, "Quiet, everybody! Stulush is going to sing us a song!"

I knew several songs—"Tumbling Tumbleweed," "Chattanooga Shoeshine Boy," "Ghost Riders in the Sky"—but my mind went blank. The band had stopped playing and people stood on the dance floor looking up at me with flushed, grinning faces. The only song I could remember was "Ol' Man River" and as I took a step backwards to belt out the first note, I accidentally kicked a couple of glasses off the table. They shattered on the floor, and instead of singing I started to cry.

"Tony, I told you, you were giving him too much to drink," Aunt Hana said.

"It's just ice water," Tony said.

"Well, *psiakrew,*" she swore, "use some common sense."

"Hey, come on, let's not start today," Tony said.

Later, when it was dark outside and the wedding was winding down, and Aunt Hana was crying while my mother consoled her, I started sneaking glasses off the table, slipping out through a side door that opened onto an alley and hurling them as if they were hand grenades. I could hear them in the dark exploding against the concrete.

Like the stories Dzia-dzia told, my memories from back then are incomplete—like fragments of dreams. I can still vividly recall throwing highball glasses down an alley, and yet, except for the conversation of my aunts and uncles at Bishop's Chili, I don't remember Dzia-dzia's wake or funeral—not the sight of him in a casket, although he would probably have been the first dead person I'd ever seen, not the requiem mass or the graveside ceremony at Saint Adelbert's, the cemetery far out on the northwest side, where most of the family is buried. I do remember eating, at Bishop's, chili mac sprinkled with oyster crackers. There were little bowls of the crackers on each table and clear bottles of hot sauce that were stuffed with floating chili peppers—but I don't recall anyone grieving, certainly not in the way we all did when, many years later, my grandmother died. Whatever they felt toward my grandfather was too complicated for me to understand, perhaps too complicated for them to articulate, and also too private. And like most private things it took the shape of silence. In place of grief, which is a form of memory, there was a silence about Dzia-dzia left behind that became a form of forgetting. So little about him had been known to begin with, and it was all far away and already seemed so long ago, as if what was in the Old

Country was automatically too old to be important in the day-to-day struggle to survive. What did it finally matter who his parents were, what place he'd come from, what his life was like before he'd come to America? Hadn't he by his own choice left that life behind? All that made up the man was the man himself, and when he vanished what was left was a few photographs and the stories, which were no longer retold. Except for my cousin Barbara, who was born shortly after I was, none of the numerous cousins who would come later ever knew him, and if Dzia-dzia was a presence at any of the frequent family parties—the Christmases, birthdays, Christenings, First Communions, and graduations—I never sensed it.

A few years after his death, although I still remembered the story about my Dzia-dzia's being buried alive, I too maintained that silence when Sister Jerome asked if anyone knew anything about coal mining. Our third-grade class was going on a field trip to the Museum of Science and Industry, where there was a famous model coal mine. You boarded an elevator that carried you like a miner down a dark shaft to tunnels winding under the earth. Kids talked reverently about it, as if we were going on a roller-coaster ride at Riverview Amusement Park rather than to an exhibit at a museum. But it wasn't excitement about the prospect of actually descending underground that I felt as much as a growing anxiety.

To prepare for the trip we studied a unit on coal—its prehistoric origins, its economic importance, and the way it was mined. What most captured my imagination was the canary. I had never heard before how canaries were kept in mines, not to sing to the miners but because canaries were more sensitive than human beings to poisonous gas. If poisonous gas seeped into the shaft, the canary's death would alert the miners. I wondered if there had been a canary in the mine at Johnstown, Pennsylvania.

Through the entire unit on coal, I never raised my hand to tell my grandfather's story. I didn't try to explain to the class that if not for coal, our family might never have moved from Pennsylvania to Chicago; Aunt Hana would have never met Uncle Tony; or, for that matter, my mother would have never met my father and I'd have never been born. And even if I had managed to be born, my fate would have been to work in the mines. Instead of studying about coal, I might have been down there already with a lantern on my forehead and a pickaxe in my hands.

The longer we studied about coal, the less I wanted to go on the field trip. Coal mining seemed more like suffering than labor—a grinding, dirty job. It was an impression I'd already formed just from watching the coal delivery men in our neighborhood. Like the garbage men and the men who delivered blocks of ice to taverns, they were mostly blacks or foreigners who rode through the alleys in big trucks. The coal trucks would back over the curb and dump a heap of coal on the sidewalk and the men would stand shoveling it through sooty little basement windows down a chute. Sometimes, in winter, I'd pass a coal delivery man down a narrow gangway hauling a bushel of coal on his shoulder, his coveralls smeared black and the whites of his eyes staring from his blackened face like those of coal miners in photographs. He trailed black footsteps in the snow.

It was the canary I sympathized with. If it was bad enough to simply be caged, how much worse to be caged underground, separated forever from the sun, whose very color a canary's feathers emulated. The only light there was a bare bulb filmed with coal dust, and the canary would whistle his song down tunnels pounding with jackhammers and the boring of drills. It seemed to me a life that was unbearably sad.

Sitting at my desk, listening to the nun talking about black lung disease, I imagined myself descending the elevator into the mine. Each shift I'd sneak something for the canary: a piece of apple, cuttlebone, a mirror, a trapeze. The foreman would observe me doing this. At first, it annoyed him, but later he decided to reassign me to the canary watch. It was a job that made the other miners resent me. It meant no more drilling, no more squirming through the wet black crevices on my belly to pick at the crumbling walls that might collapse in on me at any moment. Instead of a lantern headgear and coveralls stiff with coal dust, they made me wear a bright yellow raincoat. My job was to watch the canary, to never allow my attention to waver, to stare at him so closely that I would see the moment when he suddenly tottered and dropped from his trapeze in the middle of his song. Then I would be the one who would run through the dark tunnels yelling from the depth of my lungs, "The canary is dead! The canary is dead!"

On the day of our field trip, I pretended to be too ill to go to school. As the day progressed, my fake fever felt increasingly real until I was hot and sick to my stomach. A generation removed from the mine catastrophe that had reshaped the lives of our family, I had nonetheless inherited a sense of claustrophobia. As for the recollection of my Dzia-dzia, by then my memory of him had already turned into imagination.

Marion Bachrach Fisch

MARION WINIK

I was flipping through a copy of *Rolling Stone* magazine one sultry New Jersey summer afternoon when my dear grandmother Gigi finally remembered to tell me that its founder and publisher, Jann Wenner, was my cousin. I stared at her in shock. My cousin? How? Gigi explained that Jann's mother, Sim Wenner, was first cousin to my grandfather. Papa? I looked over at my ancient relative, snoozing in a nearby lounge chair behind green-lensed sunglasses, gray hairs curling on his weathered chest. Papa—our blood connection to the Beautiful People. Who knew?

Up until that summer, I believed myself sprung from the loins of a stolid line of businessmen and accountants, a family of ever-more assimilated Jews who had come to rest, by 1960, in various suburban outposts north and south of New York City. Mine was a nice, normal family, at least in my twelve-year-old view, and this disappointed me deeply. I wanted a gothic family, an extraordinary family, a family distinguished by personality and achievement. The fact that my mother was ladies' golf champion at her club several years running did not do it for me. My father, though a character in his own right, was not famous, fabulously wealthy, or in any way exotic. My doting grandparents, my pretty aunts and jokey uncles—all very gemütlich, thank you, but hardly the raw stuff of greatness.

Perhaps sensing that relatives with whom one has quotidian social contact are bound to remain depressingly life-size, I had begun to seek beyond the members of the Winik and Fisch clans I knew personally to unearth the towering, romantic relations I craved. Endlessly pestering my elders with leading questions and half-baked suppositions (God forbid I should read in the newspaper about anyone whose last name had more than three letters matching ours), I repopulated, reorganized, and generally spruced up our kinfolk with a host of illustrious, if absentee, additions. As it turned out, the old genealogy offered some decent raw material for my embroidery project, and my overactive imagination supplied the shiny thread.

Shortly before the *Rolling Stone* incident, my sister and I had been up one night entertaining ourselves by watching old home movies on the wall of the den. The heavy iron projector roared and ticked as backyard birthday parties and seaside romps flickered by. Then, at the bottom of the carton, we found a film unlike the others: instead of being a small plastic reel in a yellow Kodak box, it was at least a foot in diameter, stored in a cylindrical tin case labeled in spidery ink faded past legibility. When Nancy loaded it up, it turned out to be old-timey black-and-white footage in the classic silent movie style, with title cards printed in curlicued serif type. "Mr. Winik and the Kid at the Palace," said one of them. Which Mr. Winik? Which Kid? It was London, that was for sure, and there were groups of men in bowlers posed in various postcard-style settings. There was a mustache that looked strangely familiar. I could hardly sleep that night.

I learned the next morning that my great-grandfather Hyman Winik had had business connections with the Great Charlie Chaplin. (It was important to refer to him as the Great Charlie Chaplin when conveying the story to preadolescent peers.) A carpenter who fled Latvia to escape Cossack pogroms, Hyman made his fortune by traveling the world in the wake of war and natural disaster, where the need to rebuild guaranteed plenty of work. Hyman wound up in San Francisco after the Great Earthquake at the start of this century, having by then acquired an Australian wife and sons born on four separate continents. He became fascinated by the newly invented nickelodeon and opened a little theater of his own.

Through a series of lucky breaks, Hyman acquired the rights to distribute Charlie Chaplin's films, and at this point things became very glamorous: trips back and forth to London, a private screening for the queen herself, hobnobbing with the fashionable gents I had seen in the film. But the end of the story was tragic: Great-Grandpa fell out with Chaplin, who sued him for the unheard-of sum of a quarter of a million dollars, contributing to his breakdown and death before the age of fifty. Too callow to see the heartbreak in this, I saw showbiz, globetrotting, tabloid-level litigation—the sort of Winik I could proudly claim.

From then on, Spanish moss grew thick on our family tree. "My great-grandfather was the Great Charlie Chaplin's agent,"

I announced whenever possible, "and my cousin owns *Rolling Stone* magazine." My audience was usually impressed more by the latter than the former, and I saw no need to clarify the fact that Jann—I still feel I can call him that—was my third cousin, twice removed, and that I had never laid eyes on or spoken to him in my life. I assumed I soon would, as a matter of course, once I began my career as a famous rock star and novelist.

Alas, Jann has proved to be much more useful as a conversation piece than a connection; the hopeful missives I addressed to him in my late teens and twenties were answered only once, rather gruffly. But by then I had realized I didn't need to meet Jann at all, just as I didn't have to actually know Charlie Chaplin, or even Oona or Geraldine. We're talking mythology here, not kaffeeklatsch.

With Jann and Charlie playing Zeus and Saturn, I went on to cast the supporting characters of Mount Olympus. In the entertainment world alone, our genetic cosmos fairly sparkled with stars. Gigi herself once dated Richard Rodgers, of Rodgers and Hammerstein, an older boy who wrote songs for her high school musicals. My great-aunt Ethel, Gigi's sister, sang on Broadway. My step-grandmother on my mother's side was a Rockette. And wasn't it entirely possible that my mother's grandmother, Flora Arnstein, was somehow related to Nicky Arnstein, the sexy gambler who married Fanny Brice? I was sure when I saw the movie *Funny Girl* that it had to be. Mom said no, but how could she know for sure? Even if the only evidence was the powerful identification I felt with the glamorous, tragic figures played by Barbra Streisand and Omar Sharif, it couldn't be ruled out entirely, could it? (I think in some versions of this story, I was distantly related, by the transitive property of celebrity, to Streisand and Sharif themselves.)

In the sphere of public service, I somehow gathered we were connected to the famous assassinated New York liberal Allard Lowenstein. My mother, always the skeptic, insisted I had confused him with Alan Lowenstein, our dentist's brother. It turns out, actually, it was Al Blumenthal that my father's first cousin had married, the one who was president of the New York State Assembly before he went into private practice. Lowenstein, Blumenthal, whatever. The fact is, during my college years I was twice mistaken for Caroline Kennedy.

The unmet relative who is closest to me, both by bloodline and inclination, died shortly before my birth. I am named for her. My mother's mother, Marion Bachrach Fisch, may not have been famous, but lived her life on a passionate scale, defying social mores and giving all for love in a way I found mesmerizing. In the nineteen-thirties, women didn't pursue romance to its tragic end, didn't leave their husbands for their lovers, didn't marry and divorce the same man twice, didn't conduct their personal affairs with reckless intensity and disregard for public opinion and even private feelings. Except for my grandmother.

As I uncovered the story of these long-dead grandparents, Roy and Marion, I realized I had a virtual F. Scott and Zelda on my hands. She, a stunning beauty with seaglass eyes and terrific cheekbones, fell in love with a family friend named Smith and left her husband and three girls to run off with him to Washington, D.C. Furious, her husband and father conspired to prevent her from getting her hands on either her money or her daughters. But shortly after Marion married Smith and gave him a son, the man died. Distraught, she fell into the waiting arms of her ex-husband. Their second marriage to each other was brief; soon she'd moved out again, and Roy was dating the aforementioned Rockette.

By this time, my mother was grown and about to be married to my father. After the wedding, she spent "two years trying not to get pregnant and the next four years trying to," as she ruefully explains. Desperate, she sought the advice of her elegant, world-wise mother, who escorted her around New York to the latest fertility experts. The day she finally went to Marion's apartment to announce the success of the endeavor, she found her mother dead of a heart attack on the floor. Seven months later, I was born.

At nineteen, I wrote a long narrative poem about Marion and Roy, adding just a few spurious dramatic effects and gratuitously saddling everyone with Fitzgerald-size drinking problems. When I read my poem to my mother and her sisters at some holiday gathering, they all burst into tears. I took this as a good sign. I saw their weeping as testimony to my prodigious powers of insight and language, though in retrospect I wonder if they weren't just appalled.

Twenty years later, I no longer believe that suffering is glamorous, though I still think it's worth writing about, and the family that once seemed so impregnably, boringly happy to me has had its full share of domestic drama, bereavement, and pain. I have shed the illusion that famous people are automatically interesting, or vice versa, and do not tell new acquaintances I'm related to Fanny Brice. As for Marion, I now see her story is sad and even worrisome, though I can't help but take it as a compliment when my mother says I have exactly her eyes.

These days, my eyes are fixed on the road ahead, figuratively and literally: I spend a good deal of time ferrying carloads of children around the medium-sized Texas city where we live. From the backseat, that cauldron of myth, I hear awesome tales of an aunt who played professional tennis, the family fireman or figure skater, Herculean cousins, valiant pets, billionaire uncles. Because youth craves heroes, the stories continue, the apocrypha flourish. When they ask, I guess I'll dust off Chaplin, Wenner, Rodgers, and Blumenthal and see if any of them still has what it takes to fly.

As for me, I don't care about celebrities anymore as much as I do these kids; I confine my bragging to their soccer goals and art projects, their poems and spelling tests. Their future is more important to me than any past, glittering or otherwise, and I finally understand why grown-ups drink to health and security, not fame and fortune. Glamorous relatives and their lustrous achievements are dust to me now: I don't need a claim to fame, but a claim to joy.

ABOVE LEFT:
The McDonalds

ABOVE RIGHT:
Edward Morley

LEFT: *Martin
Hoagland*

EDWARD HOAGLAND

I n my late thirties I hit my stride as a writer, as many do, and caught my second wind. Earlier, I had published three novels, but I was stalled on the fourth and in the meantime had discovered essay writing through the vehicle of a long travel journal, *Notes from the Century Before,* which I had published in 1969, about the old men of Telegraph Creek, a frontier hamlet on the Stikine River eight hundred miles north of Vancouver, British Columbia.

Wilds had intrigued me since my teens, when I had ridden horseback in the Wind River Range in Wyoming, then fought forest fires in the Santa Ana Mountains in California another summer, and joined the Ringling Bros. and Barnum & Bailey Circus for two spells of caring for the menagerie cats. I'd written a successful novel about that latter experience; another, less vivid, about New York boxing; and a third, about a Pied Piper in a welfare hotel. Fiction was my first love—I had wanted to be the great American novelist—but I lacked the exceptional memory novelists need. (Montaigne, in his essay "On Liars," says he found "scarcely a trace of it" in himself: "I do not believe there is another man in the world so hideously lacking.") Perhaps as a result, I had focused upon honing a poetic style, which is an inadequate substitute. Still, as Montaigne adds, a weak memory makes you think for yourself—you can't remember what other people have written or said.

Essays, though sprinkled with subordinated memories, are written mostly in the present tense and aren't primarily narratives. The point the essayist is trying to illustrate takes precedence over his "story." The other obvious handicap I'd been laboring under in trying to become a great novelist was my disbelief that life *has* many narratives. I think life seldom works in blocks of related events. Rather, you can break your fingernails trying to undo the knots and they will stay knots. My sister and her last husband lived next to each other in isolated farmhouses without speaking for years, she with the children and the fields they'd worked, he as a hired man on other people's land. Like any rural residents, they both owned guns, and so if this were fiction their rancid feelings would finally have erupted into gunfire, arson, flight, or nervous collapse. But life is usually stasis, not a narrative; sadness, not a story. Like a car that won't start, it just won't start.

Yet my main reason for turning into an essayist had less to do with mnemonic deficiencies or any theory of life as connected to fiction than with the painful fact that I stuttered so badly that writing essays was my best chance to talk. Is *this*, therefore, maybe a story? Well, because it afflicted me so soon—and because it seems to stem from a gene passed down from an uncle of mine who also stuttered, until he died under the wheels of a Kansas City trolley car before my father's eyes at the age of nine—the idea hasn't too much novelistic interest, unless you count the wringing-out effect of the sight on my father, who later made me suffer; which to me is an essay. Just as I didn't know the great-grandmother on my mother's side, from whom I probably inherited my bad eyesight, I never knew that stuttering uncle. I have only seen his photo, where he stands next to my father, both of them in Indian headdresses and buckskin suits.

Their sister had died of blackwater fever at the age of three in a cypress swamp where my grandfather, out of medical school, had taken a job as a contract doctor. Those deep-forest, Spanish-moss swamps of Louisiana, where I've since paddled and camped with Cajun trappers, are spellbinding, larger than life, with gators, panthers, spoonbills, and storks, plus legends African, French, Attakapau. But after the death of two of his three children, my grandfather forswore further adventures and remained an obstetrician back in Missouri till the First World War. He did not see action (his own father and father-in-law had fought on opposite sides of the Civil War) but enjoyed the comradeship of army life so much that he stayed in the reserves for the next twenty years, rising to lieutenant colonel in the medical corps. After his wife's death from cancer at fifty-nine, he retired from active practice in Kansas City and quietly managed a rental property he'd invested in. He was a member of the Ivanhoe Masonic Lodge, the Modern Woodmen of America, and the Sanford Brown post of the American Legion. He sang in the choir of St. Paul's Reformed Church, took a flier in a few West

Texas dry-hole oil leases, and died suddenly of meningitis at sixty-seven in 1940 with an estate of $5,000, which is all the Depression had left him.

My father, though a blue-chip lawyer (in the semi-military phase of his own career, when he worked as a negotiator for the Defense Department in Europe, his rank was the civilian equivalent of major general), shared with my grandfather that ambiguity about their chosen professions, likewise retiring early, in his case to try to become a business-school professor and memoir writer. But my father's overly methodical cast of mind did not fit either vocation, and cancer meanly overwhelmed him at sixty-three. His adventuresomeness, instead of heading him from Kansas City to Louisiana, Texas, and a military uniform, had led him east to Yale, Wall Street, and Europe to explore the museums, restaurants, splendid scenery, the history and social complexity, Berlin, London, the Parthenon, the Grand Canal. We once crossed paths at the Trevi Fountain in Rome and had supper together, and to the pretty music of its plash he told me that "an enemy" of his had lived in this square during his period as a U.S. negotiator ten years before. But, with characteristic discretion, he refused to specify who had won or whether his adversary had been a personal rival or an outside foe of the United States.

Both he and my grandfather were genially clubby, easing their hearts among groups of men more easily than I, though perhaps not as inclined to close confidences. Nerdy, squirrelly, yet bold enough within the sphere of a loner, I was leery of the extended compromises membership entails, and maybe too odd to make them. But the professed purpose of my solitude was to speak to loads of people.

. . .

My great-grandfather Martin Hoagland, 1843–1926, of "Holland Dutch" descent, as it used to be said, to distinguish Dutch
from Germans, who were called "Pennsylvania Dutch," was
born on a farm in Bardolph, Illinois, and enlisted as a private in
the 57th Illinois Infantry regiment in 1861, mustering out as a
lieutenant in 1865 after service at Shiloh under Grant and the
battles for Atlanta and Savannah and up through both Carolinas
under Sherman. At eighteen he had been shipped from Chicago
almost straight to Shiloh. Soon after his discharge he married
Emma Jane McPhey, she being an orphan from Yellow Creek,
Ohio, raised by a Bardolph uncle and aunt, and they bought a
farm in Bardolph. But in 1871, with three of what would wind
up being seven children, they set out by Conestoga wagon for
central Kansas, settling on a soldier's homestead claim on Brandy
Lake in the Arkansas River valley, digging a sod house, the westernmost then, said his front-page banner-headline obituary in
the *Hutchinson Herald* fifty-five years later.

There were buffalo and Indians about, and he picked up
some cash by hauling supplies for Atchison, Topeka & Santa Fe
Railway construction crews as they crossed Kansas for the second cross-continental link-up in 1881. But his major enthusiasm
was in becoming a Johnny Appleseed to this dry region, bringing in apples and peaches, the first to be grown in central Kansas,
and carrying the fruiting branches to other farms to show it
could be done. He shipped some fruit to the U.S. Centennial
Exposition in Philadelphia in 1876 and became a crop reporter
for the Department of Agriculture, remaining so for half a century. He learned irrigation techniques with windmill wells, grew

the first local sorghum, timothy, and "rice wheat" (the "Turkey Red" wheat that made Kansas famous was introduced by Russian Mennonites at about the same time), and brought in Berkshire hogs and Cherokee milk cows. In the 1880s he entered the meat-and-grain business in the new city of Hutchinson, opened a clothing store, and later served as town councilman, street commissioner, police judge. But my grandfather was born in that sod house, and in my travels over a couple of decades to the Yukon, British Columbia, and Alaska I may have been in search of just this patriarch.

Ah, you might say, a multigenerational novel—but I don't think so. My father went east to become an attorney for an international oil company, others of his generation ended up with cog jobs in the white suburbs of Los Angeles, and I know of no gunfire, epiphanies, or deathbed conversions among them. To me they illustrate the flattening of the earth more than a story line; the Atchison, Topeka & Santa Fe as a bureaucracy, agribusiness monoculture replacing individual Johnny Appleseeds. I've written about John Chapman of the Ohio frontier, the ascetic saint who was the real Johnny Appleseed, and he is, in fact, an exemplar of the benign, pacific nature of a majority of the early pioneers.

I've sought frontiersmen in the river drainages of the taiga country—the least accessible country on the continent and thus last to be settled—and these people were growing parsnips and potatoes, keeping bees and chickens, coaxing peas and lettuce, storing carrots and turnips. Their pride was in their carpentry, not gunsmithing, in getting half a dozen Herefords or packhorses through the winter on the resources of a beaver meadow, not in reaming their neighbor out of five hundred bucks. I've stood at so many trail ends and hollered greetings to a log cabin set in a rough, stumpy clearing a hundred yards away, lest the person living there be startled by me, that I feel confident I know what pioneers on the frontier elsewhere were like.

These weren't gunslingers or deal hustlers; they were generally peaceable, fairly balanced souls who liked the sound of a stream outdoors, planted flower beds in front and a rhubarb patch. If they were placer miners and had found a pocket of gold grains in an old creek bed, instead of going out for a whoopee spree and never coming back, they just worked the spot and bought new stuff for the cabin (a zinc sink, an iron stove that didn't have holes in it, a mattress that hadn't yet become a hive for mice) or more hydraulic equipment, and a truck, a boat, a snowmobile to haul and float and sled it in. They, of course, were throwbacks, not ordinary people, having chosen to leave the loop of suburban malls for a riverbank. But ordinary folk did not leave the loop in Europe and come to America in the first place—or then leave the seaboard for Sioux country, living off the land, not in a money economy. Their guns were like our wallets, having the purpose of procuring food, and were not a penis or a fetish.

These people whom I'd sit with for an evening were content to watch the fire flicker in the stove and the flame of a kerosene lamp or a miner's candle for entertainment, though they might have a bit of corn whiskey too, or birch syrup, apple champagne or plum brandy, huckleberry muffins or home-pulled taffy for a treat. Water diverted from a brook ran forever through a food cooler into the sink, and a fire burned continually no matter what the weather was—these were the constants during the summer, when they dressed more warmly, and in the winter, when they dressed more lightly, than I. Their fires of regret were banked, their eyes lacked my squint under the open sky, and they didn't wish for sharp divergences from day to day, as I tend to. They were subjects for an essay, in other words, more than for fiction.

My grandmother on my mother's side collected bowlfuls of used tin-foil and balls of broken string, wrote letters to her friends on scraps of paper, and, whenever she traveled by ship or train, organized her suitcase so tightly, with her socks and foot medications at one end and her face cream and hair net at the other, that she could unpack in the dark. She would carry a dozen magazines on a trip, with the advertisements already torn out to save on weight, but, because she thought that only natural light was good for the eyes, would put her reading material away as night fell. Though she was an enthusiastic walker, the foot medications were necessary to ease her discomfort because her toes had been crushed out of shape by wearing borrowed shoes when she was a child. Her parents were pauperized by the panic of 1873, when the small-town bank they owned in Homer, New York, failed. Her uncle had been handsomely painted by Abraham Lincoln's principal portraitist, but under the weight of this disgraceful calamity her father wasted away, and after his death she and her sister and brother and mother were forced to creep to Flint, Michigan, and move in with cousins, whose shoes she wore.

So *here's* a story, you may say. Elizabeth limps on her crushed toes in hand-me-down footwear as a poor relation after her father's business failure. Then she becomes a schoolteacher and marries a businessman, A. J. Morley, after his first wife—one of her prosperous cousins, and also a teacher—dies in childbirth. They move first to Chicago, where he manages his family's wholesale saddlery store, and then to Grays Harbor in Washington State, where around 1905, he buys with Morley family money (the family was so conservative that they declined, right there in Flint, to invest in the start-up of General Motors, and later, in Washington State, were to refuse to bet on Boeing) seven thousand acres of old-growth forestland on Delezene Creek and launches a logging and shingle-mill operation in Douglas fir country. For saddlery people from Michigan who were expanding into the general hardware business, to participate also in this last hurrah of pioneering in the American Northwest was gambling of an appealingly conservative variety; and besides, they were chasing bad money with good, because A. J.'s scampish older brother Walter (later to be dragooned into the ministry as penance) had already gone west to Grays Harbor and fouled up among the con men on F Street and the brothels on Hume Street and Heron Street in Aberdeen.

A. J. was successful; yet my grandmother continued to save slivers of soap and yesterday's bread. You could cast this as a story, but I wouldn't. To me what's interesting about my grandmother is how, for example, after those virgin hemlocks, firs, and spruces had paid for her to sail to Europe with a grown granddaughter who was honeymooning, and the couple were in Rome and she was in Florence and she wished to rejoin them before the plan called for it, she simply entrained for Rome, took a taxi to the Forum, and sat down on a ruin, figuring any tourist, even honeymooners, would soon go there. Sure enough, within an hour they showed up. My mother, whose childhood was sunnier, enjoyed this commanding sort of confidence too.

But Grandfather, as his four children grew up and went east

to school (he believed, quite sensibly, that eastern children should come west for summer jobs and western children should travel east for social skills and book learning), took a mistress or two, in the fashion of a logging baron in a salmon-canning and raw, tall-timber town of four thousand people on the wild Pacific in the 1920s—though for this role, as well, he preferred the local schoolteachers to the bar girls who'd gotten Walter into trouble. Grandmother's response was to travel extensively, with or without younger companions, on cruise ships and museum tours, or else, less happily, to check into the Aberdeen General Hospital for a week's rest. One time, returning from abroad, she discovered a red nightgown hanging in her closet and thought up a better solution. Instead of fleeing to the hospital, she washed it and wore it every night until it was threadbare, never mentioning why to her husband or telling her sons about the incident until they were driving her home from their father's funeral, twenty years later.

Flamboyance, poignancy, oddity, drama, and cause and effect are all present in some modest measure, but not, I think, *plot,* in her "story." I do have another ancestor, Reuben Hitchcock Morley, a "writer/traveler," who was murdered by a traveling companion in Mongolia en route to the Russo-Japanese War in 1905. Two years before that, Benjamin Franklin Morley had lost his life in his own gold mine in Buena Vista, Colorado, and in 1942 a cousin of my mother's named John Morley died on the Bataan death march. Reuben had fought in the Spanish-American War and lived among the Yaqui Indians of Mexico and the Igorot tribespeople in the Philippines. But much more often I see life as being slower, flatter, more draggy and anticlimactic, repetitive and yet random, perhaps briefly staccato but then limpid, than all but a handful of novels, and these not the best.

I love great fiction. More than the essays of Montaigne, fiction rivets, inspires, sticks in the mind, makes life seem worth living if ever it doesn't. Novels when upliftingly tragic or vivid with verisimilitude can be unforgettably gripping. But I don't find my own life in many of them. That is, for instance, I wouldn't have married Madame Bovary or shipped out with Ahab. My life has not been Joseph Andrew's, David Copperfield's, or Raskolnikov's. I will always remember such characters, but my own marital blunders, childhood collisions, career nicks and scrapes, and even my chthonic exaltation on certain radiant days when stretching my legs out-of-doors are not synchronous with those that are plumbed in what we call masterpieces. Like Prince Andrey after the battle of Austerlitz in *War and Peace,* I've lain on my back gazing into the sky—but not so near death or to quite the same end. I'm convinced by his feelings and have known their like fitfully after quick bouts with blindness, suicidal impulses, and so on. But if mine were really the same, I'd have ceased, with Buddhist resignation, to write books.

Instead of the breakneck conundrums and rapturous gambits of some of the novels I love, it is the business of essays to be more familiar, unassuming, humdrum. The Declaration of Independence was also an essay, but there aren't many of these; and when I am miffed with my sister, at sixes and sevens with my mother, groping for an intelligent (as distinct from blind) empathy with my daughter, or tangling with the woman I presently share my life with, I'd as soon read a first-rate collection of essays for guidance as *Anna Karenina*. The personal essay is meant to be like a household implement, a frying pan hanging from a punchboard, or a chat at the kitchen table, though it need not remain domestic; it can become anguished, confessional, iconoclastic, or veer from comfortable wit to mastectomy, chemotherapy, and visions of death, just as the talk in a parlor does. Essayists are ambidextrous, not glamorous; switch-hitters going for the single, not the home run. They're character actors, not superstars. They plug along in a modest manner (if any writer can be called modest), piling up masonry incrementally, not trying for the Taj Mahal like an ambitious novelist.

"Trifles make the sum of life," said David Copperfield; and novelists and essayists share that principle. A book is chambered like a beehive, and prose is like comb honey—honey sweeter (to its devotees) because it has its wax still on. Going the other way, from fifteen years of essay writing to doing a novel again, can be exhilarating, as I later found, because one is inventing, not simply recording, the world. I could myth-make a little, draw things a bit differently from how they were, grab for the brass ring, go larger than life, escape the nitty-gritty of reality for a while. Novelists want the site of their drama to be ground zero, but most of us do not live at ground zero. Most of us live like stand-up comedians on a vaudeville stage—the way an essayist does—by our humble wits, messing up, swallowing an aspirin, knowing Hollywood won't call, thinking no one we love will die today, just another day of sunshine and rain.

BOB SHACOCHIS

For the past eight years, while America cried crocodile tears over the apparent dissolution of its families, my wife and I knocked our heads against emotional and physiological brick walls, trying to manufacture a family of our own. We have tried our very best to heed Babe Ruth's stalwart advice, "Never let the fear of striking out get in your way," but if baby-making were baseball, I'm afraid our team is playing its final season, and the game is all but over.

Back in the early eighties, when I was thirty, thirty-one, I looked around our rented Iowa farmhouse and said to myself, *There's the wife, there's the dog, where's the kid?* My wife, however, for her own irrefutably good reasons, had decided to steer clear of pregnancy until further notice, date and circumstances unspecified, at which time the subject of children would be resolved, or so it was hoped.

The rationales for having a kid—beyond the increasingly bad moral premise of the biblical command to go forth and multiply—all seemed primitive and murky to me, or pathetically selfish, sentimental, and deluded. The personification of love, the biological imperative of the species—these are tricky motives, prone to vicious paradox. My joy in watching a miniature version of my wife crawling around the house, eating out of the dogs' bowls, as she herself had done as a toddler, would surely be ineffable, and yet . . . yet what? That's just one scenario, albeit the ideal; one variation on the theme of parenthood.

Honestly, I wanted a kid and, though I had my preference, didn't feel entirely obligated to any given set of particulars. I was under the impression that progeny was a vital clause in the contract, not necessarily between men and women, but between an individual and life, a millennia-old game of tag leading back to whatever divine hole humanity had popped out of. Not that you were a deadbeat if you didn't stick to the plan—not at all. I didn't postulate procreation as the be-all and end-all of an individual's existence, but I did think it was a profound and marvelous opportunity, and why drive past a major must-see attraction on the suggested tour? Why not order everything on the house menu and be prepared to take what you get, eat what you can, and then move on, because somebody else was waiting for your seat?

As the years passed—the Year of the Pill, the Year of No Insurance, the Year of the Sterile Peanut Butter Jar, the Year of Corrective Surgery—it became increasingly evident to me that my desire for offspring coincided with my first breaks as a writer and was no coincidence at all. My literary and biological clocks were set to the same mean time. I had begun publishing—"leaving a trace," as Charlie Baxter would say—but for whom exactly? If a big part of the answer was "future generations," that meant your children but not mine, because they didn't exist out-side of my imagination. I was stripping myself bare in a rather durable form, and, for reasons selfish and vain, I felt enormous envy for my invisible heirs. Into the silence that haunts the dis-tance between a parent and a child would roar the hurricane of language that was my writing, and I wanted to observe—or at least contemplate—that dynamic of the flesh and the word, since I had inherited only the scantest record of my peasant an-cestors, and even my own parents were, and have never much attempted to be anything but, strangers to me. Parents, period—ultimately a forgivable shortcoming.

Kids as a metaphor for immortality was a soothing thought but existentially moot, and wanting children was just a wish—not a demand or an obsession, not an emergency, not an ab-solute need, especially in light of the modern devaluation of innocents. Life, I must confess, had gone on splendidly without them, and my wife and I seemed to have a tacit agreement to wait and see what happened, what turned up in the flow, re-gardless of what either of us intended. It seemed a reasonable in-termediate stance, halfway between the promiscuity of fate and the professionalism of self-determination; the middle ground between animals and gods. Yet what my wife intended wasn't al-ways clear to me, and we floated in an illusory cloud of faith, the expectation that somehow, someday, there'd probably be a child underfoot in our lives. That an alarm clock would go off, and we'd actually, conclusively, propel ourselves into the future and mate.

It did in fact happen . . . the way sadness happens, the way it takes up permanent residence in your life. One heartbreak and then another, and then that's it: something indescribably pre-cious has receded, beyond your reach, forever.

Sooner or later, I suspected, the focus would sharpen, and so it did on Christmas Eve, 1988, when the cloud darkened, as clouds do, and burst forth with a chilling downpour of tears. My wife and I were snowed in, alone with our dog, in a backwoods cabin in the Uinta Mountains of Utah. The dog—ersatz child, surrogate son—was sick, and we were just beginning to intuit that the poor guy was dying, and I blamed myself for his condition, for selfishly removing him from the old-dog comforts of Florida to expose him to this terrible onslaught of winter. Outside, a blizzard piled snow above the roofline; we huddled in the freezing cabin, heartsick, numbed by the curtain of sorrow being drawn across my wife's favorite holiday. But my wife is tough, and she battled against the surrender of her spirit. She commanded that we cheer up, drink a bottle of good wine, be tender to each other and try to enjoy our dinner on this damaged but still special occasion, and then afterward, the Christmas treat she had been anticipating all day: we'd lie in bed together and listen to our friend Ron Carlson on public radio, reading his magical short story "The H Street Sledding Record," for Garrison Keillor's show in Minnesota. It was Ron, in fact, who had lent us the cabin, and we considered him America's poet laureate of the crosscurrent passions and pleasures of domesticity.

But as the hour approached for the broadcast, the storm worsened; the radio's reception vanished behind squalls of static. We heard Ron introduced, but then the signal faded back into the darkness, and my wife howled. She would not abide this final blow, this diabolic assault by nature on Christmas. She adored "The H Street Sledding Record" and needed to hear it in the air, resonating brightly in the cabin, restoring oxygen to our emotions. There was a copy of Ron's collection *The News of the*

World on the shelf and, inspired, she announced she would read the story herself, in ghostly tandem with Ron, out loud to the only audience she had—the brutal wind, a dying dog, and me.

And so, swaddled in a blanket, she began: The story is about a man and a woman in Salt Lake City. A husband and wife. When their daughter turned four, he got the idea to pitch horse shit up on the roof on Christmas Eve—*Hey, look, Santa's reindeers pooped on the roof!*—and even though his daughter is now eight and his wife protests that he's fostering the kid's fantasies, he plans to keep throwing the shit up there every Christmas Eve until his arms give out.

My wife continued, transported by the story. It's a law, I think, not of life but of humanity, that you must find things to believe in yourself, and this family's annual attempt at the H Street sledding ritual, became sacrosanct, and there was nothing about Christmas that the daughter now looked forward to as much as the moment when she wedged herself between her mother and father atop the sled and they accelerated into the snowy darkness. My wife kept her composure until the last two paragraphs, when her voice began to waver: *And that's about all that we said, sitting up there on Eleventh Avenue on Christmas Eve on a sled which is as old as my marriage with a brake that is as old as my daughter. Later tonight I will stand in my yard and throw this year's reindeer droppings on my very own home. I love Christmas.*

Now the snow spirals around us softly. I put my arms around my family and lift my feet onto the steering bar. We begin to slip down H Street. We are trying for the record.

There's another, final line, but my wife never got to it. Her lower lip trembled and I watched her expression contort with agony. "I want my own daughter," she said, barely able to speak.

She lifted her head from the book and looked at me, overtaken by pain, and collapsed into herself. "I want my own daughter," she stuttered. "God-God-God *damnit,* where is my little girl?" and I jumped across the room to cradle her in my arms while she exhausted herself, sobbing, into sleep. This was the Christmas when our lives gave birth to a missing person, and the immensely difficult quest to track and rescue that person, that child, from the wilderness of our shared imagination.

That was life before science, before technology, and this is a story that has counted and recounted its years, its blood cycles, begging an ending that never arrives, and so it is a small, private story about weariness and despair, but equally so a story about tenacity and hope, but mostly it has become a type of travelogue about a journey we took into the kingdom of science and beyond, although I couldn't tell you what this other place was called, the world beyond the envelope of empirical remedy, but its cities have names like Dream and Myth and Angel and Prayer.

A few weeks after we returned from Utah, we lost Tyrone, our dog, so sweet a presence, our alter ego: the purest, simplest, and most viscerally consistent reflection of our joy in togetherness. Winding the clock of our days with the intimacy of dogritual, Tyrone had been with us since the early days of our relationship. We, a childless couple, were not and had never been two—always three. I didn't expect our lives would ever be the same, I had told my wife, however incorrectly, both of us strangled by grief the breezy sun-swept day we buried him in a Florida pasture. For weeks I sat in a chair, stupefied by mourning and stupefied by the awful, intolerable emptiness of the house, and yet I thought I didn't want another dog, that maybe now was the time to seize complete freedom, take advantage of our lack of responsibility for another life, however much I savored the clarity and mechanisms of such responsibility. My wife, after allowing me to stay drunk on bereavement for a month, coaxed me back to my senses. It was time, she finally said, to rebuild.

We got a new pup, very much like securing a new chamber for one's heart, and now, implicit in my wife's domestic building code was a clause acknowledging that our relationship had been rezoned for kids. "You're sure?" I was compelled to ask. We had been together thirteen years and, after our first year, when she had told me she never wanted to be pregnant—again—and told me why, I said okay, told myself to be patient, and never pressed the issue. She was a remarkable woman, beautiful and wise and strong, an intelligent and mature woman who, as a junior in high school in the late sixties, was out of it enough to get unwittingly pregnant. This happened before *Roe v. Wade,* and her parents, as you might imagine, reacted in a manner that could not be mistaken as sympathetic. In order to have a legal abortion she had to be declared mentally unfit by not one but two psychiatrists, and so her folks dragged her off to the shrinks, then dumped her alone at Sibley Hospital in Washington, D. C. My dear girl. No one explained the procedure, no one thought to tell her what was about to happen, that the fetus was too far advanced for traditional intervention and instead would require a saline solution abortion, actually a method for inducing labor, and its result would not necessarily be immediate. The OB/GYN doctors pumped my wife, who was once this frightened girl, full of salt water, and then housed her away in a room for three days, without food or drink, waiting for her body to evict the child, which it did on the fourth day, my wife exploding as she stood talking to her roommate, her womb evacuating its voluminous contents onto the tile floor. She was sixteen years old and nearly five months pregnant. She was sixteen and alone. I never knew this girl, but I knew and loved the woman she had become, and if what had happened to the girl was something that the woman could not overcome, I understood, however helpless I felt in understanding.

Now I needed reaffirmation of her own certainty, her willingness to push off from shore into the unknown and its surprising challenges, and yeah, she answered, she was sure. For the next two years we did what, conventionally, you do: we threw away the condoms and fucked. Beyond the customary rewards of lovemaking, nothing happened, although there were subtle changes in our conjugal pattern, a density that clustered around significant days of the month. I developed a keener sense of my wife's bodily rhythm, the tempo between ovulation and menses, and now I awoke each morning to the *peep* of a digital thermometer, registering the relative scale of her heat. Without urgency, we went about our lives, conscious of our agenda but not neurotically enthralled by the process. We had set up shop, we were open for business, we had a modest goal, one customer was all it would take to measure success in our enterprise, we were frustrated but not alarmed, yet in the back of our minds and increasing in frequency was an unsettling echo.

Nothing's happening. Nothing's happening.

For baby boomers approaching middle age, conception's narrative has been revised; frolicsome screwing no longer gets the job done. The river of luck must reverse course, retrace its banks, and a couple's customary ménage à trois with science undergoes radical redefinition. And for everyone who has squandered their post-pubescent lives in contraceptive bliss, trying to dodge pregnancy, all failed attempts to conceive are, at best, ruefully ironic.

Welcome then to the land of undiagnosed fertility, where the accommodations are pricey, the food is the heavy gruel of yearning, and the locals reserve the right to make your stay miserable in countless uncanny, undignified ways. Welcome to reproductive science, with its endless promises of redemption.

We had been living in Florida only a few years; my wife needed a trustworthy gynecologist. Female friends recommended a specialist, the best available in town—let's call him Doctor Cautious—and, after a preliminary examination, which revealed no obvious cause for her inability to conceive, my wife became his patient, and I soon fell victim to the diagnostic chronology and became suspect number one, ordered to sample the male version of the small but memorable humiliations commonplace to women in the literal maintenance of their inner lives. What I mean is, I had to provide a semen specimen for analysis—acrobatically ejaculate into a jar. It's a dubious, shabby pleasure and only a champion onanist would check it out as fun. Consider the furtive shift in erotic concentration from warm fantasy to cold glass cunt, the unexpected difficulty in aiming, the instant pathos and inadequacy of the absurd specimen, definitely not a butterfly or anything remotely attractive or superficially interesting. At least in the modern quest for fertility you can produce your offering to the goddess Technologia in your own home (though a nurse on hand would be nice). Then, however, you're the pizza delivery boy, committed to chauffering these thwarted figments of an incipient imagination to the medical lab across town in half an hour or the deal's off.

Several days later, my wife rang me at home with the results, relayed to her by Doctor Cautious. On the face of it, the news was somewhat of a relief. The analysis suggested that I might be the bump in our reproductive road, a condition easily repaired. I stood accused of manufacturing a brat pack of lazy sperm, layabout lads with minimalist tendencies and a lethargic bioattitude. Disciplinary action was prescribed: I must sacrifice my cherished hot baths to the elusive future, wear boxer shorts like television dads do, ingest large doses of vitamins B and C to compensate for smoking. After ten days of ball-coddling and three more of restless chastity, I was ordered to have at it again with another peanut butter jar.

Again, I heard the results from my wife: motility up there in the big-boy range, fistfights breaking out among the albino troops, the lads clamoring like barbarians for an assault on the cervical gate, drawing DNA straws to determine who among them would thrash like chinook salmon up the fallopian headwaters.

One morning a few days later we were instructed to have sexual intercourse, after which my wife had to throw on her clothes and rush to the gynecologist's office for an appalling post-coital examination to determine if her body, reacting to my sperm, was issuing the wrong chemical signals, treating the lads like hostile invaders, but no, nothing was amiss, we were all friends here in the birth canal. Dr. Cautious was cautiously optimistic. We allowed ourselves a half dozen months of mindless normalcy, bed-wise, before we were forced again to admit the obvious, only this time the obvious resonated with unsuspected depth and darker meaning. As two halves of a projected whole, we were failing to come together, turned back from our greatest ambition as a couple. We were failing to connect, not with eternity, but with the present, the here and now, and the danger in that was a sense of self-eradication.

While Dr. Cautious stoically advised patience, my wife, tentatively at first, tried to convince him that what she felt instinctively was true—that she was walking around with a rare disease, nonsymptomatic endometriosis—and although she won this battle, she lost the war. Who would argue that one level of hell is exclusively reserved for insurance companies, medical science's border guards, who cast a beastly eye upon all would-be immigrants. Finally Dr. Cautious acquiesced to exploratory surgery, but our health insurance company responded with Las Vegas rules—if surgery identified a problem, they'd pay; if surgery was inconclusive, the money—thousands of dollars we didn't have—would have to come out of our own empty pocket. Since we weren't sure anything was wrong, the gamble seemed foolhardy indeed, but it took a full year, another year of futility, to switch our policy to a more magnanimous company.

Exploratory laparoscopy confirmed my wife's worst suspicion—the most severe class of endometriosis gummed up her reproductive tract, and fibroid tumors as well as scarring condemned her, without corrective surgery, to permanent infertility. Good news, sort of; the procedure had a high success rate, but its prep was a hormonal nightmare, my wife made to endure two months of chemically induced menopause designed to shrink the marble-size growths to facilitate their removal. The operation itself reminded me of an updated druidic ritual, ending with my wife and I viewing a videotape of her uterine wall being seared by a laser scalpel, inserted through her belly button, while Garth Brooks sang about betrayal on the OR boom box. "Look," said Dr. Cautious's laconic voice-over on the tape, "there's your gallbladder." Little wonder she had dragged her heels in her decision to procreate.

Five months later she was pronounced fit and serviceable. Six months later, she waved a little plastic stick in front of me, which it seemed she had just peed on. "Do you see a little blue line there?" she asked anxiously, pointing to a tiny indicator window on the home pregnancy test. *Is that a blue line???*"

It was.

A month later, she returned home euphoric after her first sonogram, waving the indecipherable image of a fingernail-sized fish baby—our embryonic child. I couldn't relate to the linear storm of squiggles, which seemed of secondary importance to the sea change in my wife's demeanor. She had never felt better, she claimed, she had never felt this good in all her life. I often found her on the phone, talking excitedly with her friends, her sisters, her mother, and I told her this worried me; perhaps she should wait until the end of the first trimester to spread the fantastic news, but she couldn't contain her joy, she wanted to share the hard-won moment with those who loved her, and if the unthinkable happened, then she would share the pain of that, too.

The following month, December, I was on my way to Sikkim, the Himalayan mountain state, on assignment for a magazine. I found myself in the back of a Jeep, in the pitch of night, freezing, thrown against a British tourist named Christine as the driver muscled the wheel into another hairpin turn. We were headed to the top of Tiger Hill, above the former colonial hill resort of Darjeeling in northeastern India, to wait for the sun to rise above the endless corrugations of southwestern China and burst forth over the forbidden kingdom of Bhutan. As it did so, its rays would cast a kaleidoscope of color, light, and shadow upon one of the planet's most stunning panoramas, a mammoth uplift of the earth's crust culminating in the five summits of the world's third highest mountain, and most sacred of its fourteen 8,000-meter peaks, Kanchenjunga.

The Jeep fell in line with a sluggish caravan of fellow sight-seers, our chain of headlights sweeping the mountainside as we plowed up Tiger Hill. There's so little left of the world where men and women live their lives in the luminous presence—and ominous throb—of its physical sacredness, and I had to wonder, riding up Tiger Hill, if any place remained where the sublime continued to exist unviolated; where, with some assurance, a person could invest their spirit in the world without battling the adulterations. For me, nature wasn't a metaphor or a myth informing a system of worship, but a pure interpretation of the mind of God, or, to say this another way, the force of intelligence within creation.

Yet even nature's literalness could be obscured by narrative device, outrageous symbolism, and illusion. Sometimes it was easiest to believe that the divine could be adequately approached only in the nuclear lab, counting quarks. Still, when it wasn't trying to kill you with the fury of an absolute truth, nature could always be relied upon to provide glimmerings, intimations, whiffs of consciousness—bursts of sensory phrasings that seemed freighted with meaning, but nothing too articulate, nothing that could be explicated or deconstructed into understanding. In a small boat far away from land, or walking across flat desert at twilight, or lying on your back under a night sky salted with stars, you got pretty strong clues about the character of infinity, but still they were only clues. Nothing to take to the bank.

We passed through Tiger Gate, then maneuvered our way through the observatory's parking lot to a space at the north rampart, where the world dipped away from Tiger Hill and then heaved itself, fifty miles off in the distance, up into the solar system. The predawn sky was pristine, clear, inky blue except for a faint scarlet thread of light in the east. Christine and I unfolded ourselves from the Jeep, walked the few steps to a low wall, and stood there, focusing, the cold snapping me alert. There was a half moon, and in its glow we could make out the supernatural shape of the mountain, almost opalescent, floating on clouds bivouacked throughout the valleys. Beyond Kanchenjunga, the white nose cone of Everest thrust upward, another apparition. Where we waited, the elevation was about 8,000 feet, quite high, actually, if we had been in the Colorado Rockies, but Kanchenjunga rose another 20,000 feet above us, incredibly into the heavens.

In less than ten seconds since we had left our vehicle, something extraordinary happened. As we stood and tried to comprehend the immensity of the mountain—our first true sight of it—a shooting star blazed down, remarkable in itself, but more remarkable was the fact that the star began to burn *below* Kanchenjunga's summit, streaking down at a diagonal right to left, perhaps another 5,000 feet before it was extinguished. Christine and I were speechless for a moment, and then I blurted out, without forethought, "That was about my child." I had no idea what I meant, though surely the pregnant wife I had left behind in the United States was prominent in my subconsciousness.

Twenty minutes before sunrise, Kanchenjunga was as pale and delicate as porcelain and unconditionally divine. Its slopes pinkened, then right before dawn the clouds became restless and began to levitate out of the valleys. Their interplay with the five summits was astonishingly mystical, and I preferred this hide-and-seek game to the full disclosure of a clear blue sky, since the Himalayas seemed to belong more to the universe than to humanity. Minute by minute the clouds devoured the colossus, opening and closing windows, here a marble throne room, here a sudden glistening crag of summit that doesn't make visual sense, a shard of earth broken free. Then Kanchenjunga was gone, and it was easy not to believe it was ever there.

We all descended Tiger Hill in a single roar, back to the lively city, where I fixed myself a hot bath and packed my bags for the long road trip to Gangtoc, the capital of Sikkim. I was happy, waiting for my ride under a blue sky filled with children's kites, remembering the falling star, the enigma of its message. My wife had insisted that the right to name our child was hers alone (since I'd been the one to name our dogs), but that morning I made a queer decision that the kid's middle name should be Kanchenjunga. In the days ahead I would tell the story of the shooting star to new friends in Sikkim, and they would congratulate me on the gift of such an auspicious omen. A month later I would receive letters from them at my home in Florida, prayers that all was well with the child, that my firstborn would be a son, but by then I already knew that the very morning I had seen the star flame across the face of Kanchenjunga, halfway around the world, the fetus had died and my wife was in the midst of a miscarriage.

A year later and another Christmas, another cascade of gut-wrenching tears. I was caught by surprise and sat down next to my suddenly bawling wife on the sofa, embracing her. "Honey, what's wrong?" I asked softly. "The baby died a year ago today," she wailed, choking on her grief. I didn't quite understand and stupidly asked, "What baby?" The truth was, I had never really permitted myself to imagine the child that had inhabited her womb for a scant three months, a most ephemeral bond between us, tissue thin and prematurely ruptured. I hadn't wanted to think about it as human and *there,* as real, storing away my acceptance until I saw her belly swell, until the day she placed my hand on its roundness to feel the first kick. Of course I knew the fetus had existed but, other than having the inexplicable experience on Tiger Hill, I had not connected with that existence, and for me this shadow child remained shapeless, faceless, and nameless, forever lost in the cosmic mail, something that had profoundly inspired us but had come no closer to our lives than a falling star.

But for her it was different; my wife's own blood had bled into this baby; she had acknowledged its presence in her breasts, her toes, her skin, and when its thimble of life had spilled—not a miscarriage technically but a death that would have to be cleaned away in the hospital—she had known that, too, before any doctor's confirmation. And, as the emotionally bleak and difficult new year unraveled, it became apparent that the mutuality of our journey seemed fatally threatened by the event.

There were cognitive and psychological issues I came to realize were not mine and never would be, given my gender and its biological limitations. In the ongoing rehearsals for parenthood, I was conception's silent partner, a passive investor, spermatologically speaking, while my wife was the line producer, subject to the paralyzing responsibilities of opening night. Awash in melancholy, I watched her self-esteem begin to wobble, the burden of doubt crease her face. She felt under siege by the possibility that her continuing infertility would defeat our relationship. Was she dispensable? Would I awake one morning as merciless as Henry the Eighth? These questions landed like punches on my heart, yet it was true that it became more and more difficult to conceal my dissatisfaction with the progress of the campaign. Dr. Cautious ordered more tests, but to me his stewardship seemed defined by infuriating hesitation. Let's find out where we're going and get there, I lobbied my wife. All problems ought to have solutions.

As the year went by I was often on the road, teaching, working for magazines, on a book tour, one of us parachuting in on the days she ovulated. The schedule grew tedious but there was a certain harried romance to it all. In six months we made love in Florida, London, New York, Missouri, and twice in Washington, D. C. My wife had finished law school and had anchored herself with a job, as a staff attorney for the Florida legislature, and she made no secret of her loneliness, falling asleep twenty-five out of every thirty days sandwiched by our two dogs but otherwise alone, and my guilt whispered to me, *Give her a child to keep her company.*

Instead of abandoning hope, we amended it, developing contingency plans. We began to speak about adoption matter-of-factly, with an explicit though not fully parsed understanding that we would stay the biological course, run with the trickle of our luck until the trickle itself ran dry. Adoption was and always had been our safety net and we in fact considered it a second act, a sequel; once we got rolling we were going to pack them in, fill up the house. Whenever I headed overseas, before she kissed me good-bye my wife would wistfully say, "Bring me home a baby."

Ever since I had known her, she had imagined herself the mother of a little Oriental girl. First, though, we were going to expend all biological options, like a twelve-step recovery program, one day at a time.

Late that summer I went to Haiti to cover the U.S. military intervention, and went back and forth between the island and Florida for the next eighteen months. Dr. Cautious ordered more tests; injected dye into her womb indicated a blockage of scar tissue in one fallopian tube and clear sailing in the other. Shouldn't be a problem, Dr. Cautious proclaimed. I was made to jerk off into more bottles; then there were more tests, more pale assurances. My wife was beginning to feel like a tawdry undergraduate lab experiment, and I quite frankly was getting fed up, not with her, but with Dr. Cautious.

One night I returned from Haiti and found my wife in bed, her face swollen from weeping. She didn't cry often, and never for sentimental reasons. It was her habit to put on a brave face, endure her tribulations in silence. Occasionally she'd complain in a depressed voice that her friends didn't understand her, that they thought she was tough but she wasn't, and so they failed to comfort her when she most needed their support. Once or twice a year, her suffering would overflow the cup of its solitude, and this was one of those times. One of our close friends had died in an accident, another was terminally ill, and she had just learned that her sister had breast cancer. "I've been lucky," she told me bitterly, the tears streaming down her face. "There's tragedy in every life but I've been spared. My tragedy is to have no children. I waited too long for everything."

This moment was the closest I have ever heard my wife come to self-pity. Our struggle wasn't making either of us strong, only resigned, our hearts slowed by sadness. Her words frightened me; their wretched poignancy galvanized me into action. Our advance to the next level was long overdue, and I insisted on accompanying her to a consultation with Dr. Cautious. Was I pushing this beyond her capacity and desire? No, she said, this is what she wanted, too, but no matter how much a couple discusses such things, the right and the wrong of a decision are never easily figured out or entirely resolved. At the gynecologist's office, I sat and listened to him murmur his tepid consolation, the platitudes of his profession—just keep trying, hope for the best—and I resisted the urge to leap across the desk and shake the complacency out of this well-intentioned but uninvested man. "This is no good, this is crazy, and I want it to stop," I said. I was forty-three years old, my wife was forty-two, and time was the luxury of other, younger couples. "What do you want to do?" he asked, and we left with a referral to the fertility clinic at the University of Florida.

On the morning of our appointment in the summer of '95, we drove to the Park Avenue Women's Center in Gainesville, Florida, where we sat in a waiting room filled with madonnas and infants, inhaling the postnatal smells—diapers and talcum and milky vomit—of our destiny. We were fetched to an interview room and introduced to Ginny, the personification of compassion, a nurse who would serve as our guardian and guide into the enchanted forest of in vitro fertilization. The questions were commonsense, the literature lucid and comprehensive—ovulation induction, egg retrieval, fertilization, embryo transfer; micromanipulation, egg donation, and cryopreservation. Ginny explained success rates: IVF—25.3 percent; egg donor IVF—43 percent. A roll of the dice, but "a realistic option for many infertile couples who might otherwise never become pregnant." Doc came in to scan our medical histories, cluck over our age, and close the deal. "I recommend we proceed aggressively," he said, and, despite my wife's apprehension, I seconded the motion. Ginny returned to discuss the finances—in the next five months we would empty our savings account, take out a bank loan, and beg an advance against future earnings from my literary agent. After a blood test for AIDS, while my wife was undergoing a pelvic exam I was directed to the bathroom, given tattered copies of *Playboy*—erotic white noise, and told to masturbate. It was my one genuine sacrifice, this fatuous unwanted pleasure, on the altar of fertility, a free ride compared to where my wife now stood poised, a seasoned veteran of repeated bodily invasions, on the feudal threshold of new tortures. We reunited in an examination room, where Ginny began uncapping syringes and lining up innocuous vials of saline solution. Once we had started down this road, I would be called upon to give my wife a month-long sequence of daily injections in the ass, with a needle the length of my middle finger, and now Ginny was going to train me how to do it. She demonstrated how to mix the hormones, fill the syringe, tap it free of air bubbles, jab it to the hilt into an orange. There was a pamphlet Ginny showed me, with a line drawing of a woman's backside, identifying the half-dollar-size area on each buttock that could safely receive the needle.

"Fine," I said, thinking, *Can we go now?* "Okay," said Ginny, "let's have your wife lie down and pull up her skirt." I felt a flush of vertigo and pushed it away. "You're kidding," I protested, but of course she wasn't; this was my only opportunity to get it right with the proper supervision. After I had nervously filled the syringe, as I leaned over my wife's butt with the gleaming needle

I felt the vertigo return and told Ginny I didn't want to do this. "Just plunge it straight in like a dart," Ginny coaxed, and so I did, horrified as I watched my wife grimace, her hands contract and her knuckles whiten, and as soon as I removed the needle from her flesh I lay down atop her, tears in my eyes, kissing her cheek and apologizing. Teamwork, I thought, had never been so cruel. Ginny had been a paragon of empathy, though, and I thanked her. "You have the perfect job," I said naively, "bringing so much joy into people's lives." She brightened for a minute but then her eyes turned momentarily doleful and her mouth grim. "Yes," she said, "but when it doesn't work it can be devastating."

By the end of September, we would be well educated in the exact nature and magnitude of that devastation. By mid-August I was back in Haiti and my wife began self-injecting Lupron, a fertility drug that gave her hot flashes and insomnia, into her stomach to suppress and then synchronize egg—oocytes—development in her ovaries. A few weeks later I was back home, in time to begin turning her ass into a pincushion, shooting doses of Pergonal and Metrodin, to begin stimulating egg develop-ment, into her buttocks morning and night. Neither of us was brave about the hateful needles. In Haiti I had assisted military medics in triage situations; without blinking I had stood over mangled bodies holding IV bags while the victims passed into shock and died. The sense of detachment was immediate, but, undone by the intimacy between us, I could not muster it to give my wife a simple shot, and for a month we both lived in dread of the injections. Frequent blood tests—which turned her arms black and blue—and ultrasound exams—in which she was painfully prodded by a magic wand inserted into her vagina— multiplied the Dantesque hellishness of her suffering. Finally, when her ovarian follicles had achieved the optimal size, I shot her up with a hormone to trigger ovulation, and we drove to Shands Hospital in Gainesville to be "harvested." For the second time in our lives, I impregnated my wife, although this time fertilization occurred in a petri dish, at the hands of Jack the embryologist. Two days later, four embryos, the total batch, a veritable tribe of babies mathematically, were placed inside a Teflon catheter and transferred into my wife's womb. We drove home. Twelve days later, by the time she had dragged herself to the clinic for a pregnancy test, the results were moot, because two days earlier, in a gush of tears and blood, whatever children who would ever unite our separate DNA structures, marry the essence of our flesh and blend our natures into the next generation of us, had vanished back into the unknowable starry night of eternity. We were permitted two more attempts by the wizards of reproduction, both aborted early in the game when it was clear that my wife's body would not respond to the drugs.

It seems it's always meant to be December, and I am always meant to be away, when the news that rocks the foundation of our lives arrives. I called her from Haiti and listened quietly to her ragged, fatigue-ridden voice. Ginny had phoned that afternoon to tell her that her ovarian reserve was depleted, her infertility was irreversible, she was biologically incapable of procreation, permanently exiled from the purest form of motherhood, though not from motherhood itself. We secured a second opinion from one of the pioneers in the field, and the verdict was final.

I came back home to watch my shattered wife decorate the Christmas tree, to rise early in the morning, day after day, to bake cookies for the holidays—to *bake and bake and bake and bake.* What was she going to say, use what words to describe her anguish, to tell me what was going on in her mind or in her heart, and what more could I do than promise her, with a lover's force of conviction, that another Christmas would not pass without a child in the house.

So here's how things stand.

The last Xeroxed calendar—ART OVULATION INDUCTION/ ASSISTED HATCHING—taped to the refrigerator has come down, a calendar similar to its three predecessors, each an anxious countdown through the spectrum of faith and the prosaic torment of science to the imagined felicities of maternity, and each ending with the death of hope, and it is hope, more than anything else, that my wife most fears these days. Hope's betrayal. After we have packed our bags for the trip south, I take the wishbone off the kitchen windowsill, where I had placed it the previous Thanksgiving. "It's time to cash this in," I tell my wife, but she balks, afraid that if we break the bone she'll be left with the short end, she'll be the one whose wish never comes true. "Come on," I badger her, "let's do it. You can't lose." Maybe she thinks I'm wishing for a new car or a vacation in Hawaii, instead of a chance at the H Street sledding record.

The wishbone cracks straight down the middle into equal halves. *Wow,* we tell each other. Her half goes into her purse.

The next morning we're in Gainesville, Florida, in an operating room at the university's hospital. Stainless steel, high-intensity lights, state-of-the-art computer-age electronics. Everyone's in their green surgical scrubs, including me, except for my wife, who's draped in a flimsy institutional gown, prone on the table.

Her feet are placed flat, socks keep them warm, and her legs are bent at the knees, a drape spread from one kneecap to the other, making an open-ended tent between her thighs. Her expression is upbeat—everybody's expression is upbeat—but in the far recesses of her courageous eyes, under the surface of her resilient smile, I can measure her distress, I can see the look of someone who's been persecuted over and over again, with no possibility of escape, and I am crushed by the quiet heroism of her forbearance.

The three modern faces of the stork—the doctor, Ginny the nurse coordinator, Jack the embryologist—hover over the table, gayly inspecting what my wife holds in her hand, some things, objects, icons—her fertility fetishes and good-luck charms, which she keeps in a plastic cup she made by sawing off the bottom quarter of a low-fat yogurt container. Her desperate cocktail of beliefs. There's a walnut-size clay sculpture of a Paleolithic Venus—the prototypical earth mother—sent by her ill sister in San Francisco. In a doll-size leather pouch, a saint's medal, perhaps the Virgin Mary with child, carried throughout World War II by the father of a friend who has had two IVF daughters. In a spice bottle, several grams of holy dirt, said to produce miracles of healing, that my wife the previous summer scooped from the floor of the mission chapel in Chimayo, New Mexico. (She's told me she sometimes eats a pinch or two, and, although I too believe in mysteries and believe that perhaps coincidence has a capricious mind of its own, I don't really want to hear this.) On a gold chain around her neck she wears an evil eye I brought her from Turkey, her schoolgirl confirmation cross, a medal dedicated to someone called Our Lady of Victory, a prelapsarian mosquito embedded in amber, and a small ring of happiness jade, a gift from a friend in China.

This is the frontier of neoprimitivism, of the techno-voodoo of the new millennium, and I can't resist a wisecrack. "Hey, she's even got a chicken's head from last night's sacrifice in her purse," I joke. The eyes of two technicians in the room, two black women, grow wide.

"You don't notice them pooh-poohing any of it," protests my wife.

"Whatever works," Ginny replies cheerily.

"Why not?" says the embryologist. "You don't really think we have all the answers, do you? Who knows how all of this really happens?"

Collectively, we are all trying to ignore how goddamn bizarre this is—so weird it makes me spin, the moments when I contemplate what we're doing, though I mostly try to look past the details. In my own hand I hold a questionnaire filled out by the anonymous twenty-three-year-old woman with whom, two days previously, I had test-tube sex. There is a cover page, a profile of the donor, and, on it, in Ginny's handwriting, is a statement of motivation that both intrigues and baffles me: *She wants to do something nice.* Something *nice?* The language of altruism strikes me as girlish and archaic, incongruous with the high-tech world of ovarian manipulation. The night before I had a dream about this young woman I will never meet; we sat in a room together and talked, though I can't remember what we said to each other. At breakfast, before coming to the hospital, I told my wife about the dream. "What did she look like, what color was her hair?" she asked—Ginny had told us the donor's hair was dark blond. "Not really dark blond," I said to my wife. "It had red undertones." Now, as I flip through the questionnaire, my wife places her finger on the page, pointing to a box that states the woman's hair color: strawberry blond. I think of the Himalayas, and I think of this dream woman's hair, and I know that we live in a strange and marvelous world, and that the gods are forever playful and forever without pity.

When I asked her, this was the part my wife preferred I didn't write about—not the quirky, clutching mysticism, but the enormously complicated choice of egg donorship, which neither of us had ever suspected would elicit such callous response from our closest friends. *Why would you want to do that?!* they challenged my wife on the telephone—almost invariably women with their own children, women whose souls had never been lacerated by the psychic trauma of infertility, women who will never know the toll of our quest to have what for them was so easily given. Their unthinking censorship brought out the devil in me: in my fantasies I took away their children, then proposed a deal—they could have them back, though slightly altered; they would more or less look and act as they always had, yet they would no longer possess their maternal genes. That, or never see them again. What do you suppose they'd choose? Another friend, a deliberately childless artist, a former hippie who was exploring New Age conservatism and greed as she widened into her fifties, strongly disapproved. "We're living in an age of high novelty," she complained, and broke into tears. For her dearth of compassion, this woman I would send to purgatory for a thousand years, to bone up on the history of human ingenuity.

The doctor pushes a button; above my wife's head a television monitor descends from the ceiling, and there, on the screen, in translucent cabbage-green monochromatic simplicity, are the magnified kids, in truth no larger than the molecules of ink in the very tip of my pen, poised to write the word *gestation,* the word *family*. Three perfect human embryos in colloidal suspension: one five-cell cluster and two four-cell motes that, within the next few minutes, will be implanted into my wife. I study the images with a mixture of awe and alienation. These are faeries, I suppose. Angels dancing on the head of the embryologist's pin. More idea than substance, spirits videotaped on the cusp of potentiality, not quite of this world, clinging to the slightest speck of flesh. Chimeric souls in their barest, most primary transition from nonexistence to being.

On the OR boom box, Jimmy Durante is singing "Make Someone Happy." The doctor has his head inside the tent, between my wife's legs. The embryologist approaches with a stainless steel cylinder in his hands, something that looks like a cake frosting applicator. The doctor feeds the tube's catheter past my wife's cervix, the embryologist unscrews a cap at the top of the cylinder, and gravity nudges the embryos home. "We don't want to see you coming back out of there," Jack tells the faeries, "for nine more months."

As I write these last lines, it is a Saturday afternoon, ten days later, the beginning of Memorial Day weekend, May 25, 1996. We're nervous wrecks, my wife and I. She has spent the morning sweeping the patio, then making mango sorbet and baking almond cookies for a dinner party we will host tonight. A few moments ago I asked her how she was feeling and she said, "Weird," but there's no way to gauge the significance of this, and now she has gone upstairs to lie down in bed. In two more days—on Monday—she will go to the hospital for a pregnancy test, if she can hold out that long. It was another Saturday, back in September, the tenth day in the sequence of our first in vitro attempt, that her uterus expelled the embryos.

In the newspaper this morning I read that on this day, sixty-one years ago, the great Babe Ruth hit the final home run of his career. *That's something,* I told myself, and felt another pang of encouragement, here at the end of the road.

AFTERWORD:

GEN-NARRATION

JANE SMILEY

The first novel I ever knew was our family. We had every necessary element, from the wealth of incident both domestic (my grandfather wearing his bowling shirt to my aunt's wedding because nothing else was ironed) and historical (my uncle in World War II, lying in the belly of a bomber, photographing successful destruction), to the large cast of characters—my mother and her four siblings, their husbands and wives, and many cousins, the thirteen children who made up our generation. We had geographical sweep and the requisite, for an American novel, adventure in the West: my grandfather and two of his brothers had been sent from Missouri to Idaho to ranch. From there, where grandfather and grandmother met and married, to Texas, then, with the failure of that ranch, back to Missouri and quotidian employment. My grandfather had a Fitzgeraldian glamour—a handsome and athletic Sigma Chi at the University of Missouri just before World War I, he set a pole-vaulting record there that lasted into the era of fiberglass poles. We had mythic deep background—antecedents at Jamestown, mysterious dark deeds in Tennessee, a Norwegian great-grandmother who emigrated, on her own, at sixteen. We had peripeteia glad—when my mother joined the army, she managed to find her sister's boyfriend in Paris and persuade him to write my aunt, who was languishing at home, even though he was convinced that photographing bombings would get him killed—peripeteia sad—the diamond ring my grandfather won for my grandmother in a poker game disappeared down a sink drain in the thirties—peripeteia of loss—the handwritten notes my great-grandfather the newspaperman got from Jesse James, when he was jailed in Northfield, Minnesota, were later thrown out by my great-grandmother as not worth taking when they moved to Idaho—and peripeteia of gain—the little soft drink company started by some cousins we later held in our hands in the shape of green 7-UP bottles. It had two beginnings—the day my grandmother, the new schoolteacher, came to town and my grandfather saw her was one; the day after the wedding, when my grandmother got up to wash dirty dishes accumulated over months by my grandfather and his brother was the other. Our novel had as many voices as it had characters, each eagerly contributing his or her own detail, his or her version. Our novel had a ready audience—us grandchildren; we asked for the stories, looked at the pictures, delved into the deep background. We suspended disbelief with vast willingness, invariably charmed and gratified by the most casual addition to the family novel.

Our novel had a larger meaning—its location in Saint Louis, at the confluence of the continental river system, and its interpenetration with American history from the beginning teased us in our smallness, invited us to look out, look back. My grandfather's loving renditions of many songs—"Sweet Betsy from Pike," "Oh, Shenandoah," "I Ride an Old Paint," "Lorena"— reminded us simultaneously of him and every other American experience, as did my grandmother's expressions: "mad as Tucker," "talking through his hat," "Well, that settled his hash." It was a certain kind of novel, too, a realist novel in which the tragic always gave way to the comic, which was in turn always shaded by the tragic. Any character's romantic flights were quickly and sometimes brutally terminated by the wit of the other characters. When my cousin Steve tried to import a little modernism into our novel by writing his dissertation on Ezra Pound, who came, as did my grandmother, from Hailey, Idaho, the infection failed to take. A realist to the end, my grandmother was always sure of what had happened and always ready to recount it.

Now this spring our novel has an ending, with my grandmother's death on March twentieth at ninety-seven and a half, and it also has a coda. I have just spent the weekend in Saint Louis with the rest of the family, participating in a memorial service for my grandmother, which featured eulogies by nine of her grandchildren. If we hadn't realized before this, we know now who was the heroine of our family novel.

There is a picture no one can find, which I'm sure I've seen—my grandmother at sixteen, just after the death of her father. When I remember that image, I am automatically amazed and gratified by the future that lies before her—the adventures with my dashing grandfather, the fascination of birthing and then rearing my mother and her siblings, then the crowning delight of the coming of us, her grandchildren. When I gave my talk, I wanted to begin with the sentence, "When grandmother was fifty-one, I, her favorite, was finally born." If I had, everyone would have laughed, knowing both that I wasn't the favorite (each of them was) and that grandmother had the special gift of cherishing us individually. If I think of that picture a little longer, though, I see that for her possibly the best part of her life was finished. Her beloved father had just died of Rocky Mountain spotted fever, the ironic result of his passion for the outdoors and the mountains, which she shared. My cousin Lucy, whose own father (the airborne photographer) died when she was sixteen, told us that she and grandmother had always secretly shared this bond. And the girl in this photograph wouldn't be living in the mountains all that much longer—when she was twenty-five, my grandfather and his brother signed away the ranch over her objections, and she had to live out her life, eighty more years, in a region she found uncongenial. Her longing for Idaho never left her. My cousin Steve, for whom the girl grandmother has always been the most compelling, reminded us of that.

My grandfather, who fascinated us grandchildren with a combination of force, loving attention, good looks, athletic prowess, narrative flair, and musicality that for his offspring came to define the word *masculinity* wasn't, perhaps, the best husband for her. He was hot-tempered and selfish, more at home among men than women, probably lacking in resolution and strength of character, at least compared to her. Something her father had— gentleness perhaps—her husband lacked. She did not get along well with her mother (who lived with her until she died), and yet something her mother had—sheer survivability, sheer energy, sheer coldness when needed (my great-grandmother, the sixteen-year-old immigrant, got into the habit of faking heart attacks when crossed. My grandmother got into the habit of stepping over her mother's prostrate form and going about her business)—the daughter did not lack. My sister reminded me of this when she told us about a letter my grandmother had recently sent her reminding her to stand up to the men in her life and not let them tell her what to do. Once, when I was passing through Saint Louis on my way to give a lecture, I called grandmother, and she told me for the first time about how much she, a talented musician, had loved to play the piano at dances when she was a girl. One of her bitterest regrets was that she had let my grandfather forbid her to play in public, as not suitable for a woman, his wife.

One of my aunts said to me, "Well, she may have been the perfect grandmother, but—" Her failures as a mother are no family secret. We grandchildren excuse her; her daughters do not. We say she did the best she could with her mother always underfoot, her husband always having his own way (Not!" says my mother, his partisan), five children, the Depression, Uncle Charlie, no money, the war. Oh, but the joke on the sisters was that her sons-in-law adored her, her son worshipped her with the half-joking name "Fatima," pronounced "FuhTEEMa," usually shortened to "FaTEEM," as in "Hey, Fateem, where are my socks?"

The soul of our novel, its central time period, is the fifties and the early sixties, the years when all the siblings were married and giving birth to the darling grandchildren, when we were playing with one another, listening to the stories, and becoming conscious of and constructing a novel for ourselves to live warmly inside of. All of the eulogizers allude to this period. I tell the story of the time the bad boys and I were throwing water balloons out of the front windows of the house, and one landed at her feet when she was ascending the steps heavily laden with groceries. Nancy remembers the eternal phrase, "Don't slam the screen door!" Mark recalls the cinnamon buns. Lucy remembers her lap, and the other kids sharing it. These allusions evoke layers and layers of others, ones that each of us has remembered over the years, but also ones that we've shared far from Saint Louis, over the phone, in restaurants, in one another's apartments and houses. There is one thing we are always eager to do, and that is construct the family novel. When we visited grandmother, even in her very last months, when she could barely see and hear, when she was ill and in pain, she too was still eager to construct the family novel. She too felt, I think, that as much as she lost at sixteen, what she later found was amazing, gratifying, and maybe a small compensation for her loss.

The oddest eulogy is Jody's. Jody has become Carl in manhood. He is the first-born grandchild, the tallest and the handsomest, the one who went to Vietnam in the navy as a seaman and was still there as a CPO to fire the first rockets in the Gulf War, our generation's contribution to history. His eulogy doesn't refer to us or even, it seems, to grandmother herself. It is about a woman at the top of a mountain, discarding bit by bit all the accoutrements of her life. It is a stab at evoking our grandmother's inner self, her spiritual journey, as she puts off this world, including us, and goes elsewhere. We don't know what to make of it because, I think, it fingers the mystery at the heart of our family novel—how grandmother experienced herself without us and without words. It makes us sad and impatient. We don't want to think of ourselves without her, nor of her without us. Both are too frightening.

After the service, we do what our family always does best—we have a good time. Though we can be pretty bad one on one, get us in a group and we are terrific—funny, teasing, affectionate, attentive to the children. Our only argument is about who has the best dog—someday, we vow, all the dogs will come, too, and the question will finally be decided. We keep saying that we should get together like this again, more often, every year—but where? I realize that as much as we long for one another, it can't be done. The novel is over. We have to close the cover, however reluctant we are to do so. My uncle is patriarch of his own clan—four children, nine grandchildren. Other clans have been late getting started or have broken up early. The easy familiarity and affection we grandchildren feel with one another is the one legacy we can't pass on to our children; we have to keep it for ourselves and cherish it as one of our grandmother's gifts.

When I was standing at the podium, giving my eulogy, my three-year-old son left his seat and walked up the aisle to me. His manner was conversational rather than needy. When I mentioned the balloon hitting the step and breaking, spraying her legs, he said, "Was it a spray balloon, Mama?" as if he was totally familiar with the varieties of balloons. I said that it was. He stood beside me, looking out at the group. I like to think that he was surveying his past, beginning to write his novel, assembling characters in his subconscious to live alongside the immediate, Freudian ones of Mom, Dad, sisters, and I like to think that our voices, speaking of our grandmother, entered him and lodged there, just at the boundary of conscious memory, ready to emerge when all of us are gone, and he is speaking to our unknown descendants.

ABOUT THE CONTRIBUTORS

JOSÉ RAÚL BERNARDO is the author of the novel *The Secret of the Bulls.* While still a student in Cuba, he was taken prisoner by the Castro regime because of his strong belief that people have the right to express their personal views. He was able to escape to the United States and eventually complete his education in New York City. He now lives in the Catskill Mountains in New York State.

EDWIDGE DANTICAT was born in Haiti and now lives in Brooklyn, New York. Her first novel, *Breath, Eyes, Memory,* won wide acclaim, and her collection of stories, *Krik? Krak!* was a National Book Award finalist in 1995.

BEVERLY DONOFRIO is the author of *Riding in Cars with Boys,* a memoir, and a commentator for National Public Radio. She lives in Orient, New York.

STUART DYBEK is the author of two short story collections, *The Coast of Chicago* and *Childhood & Other Neighborhoods,* and a book of poems, *Brass Knuckles.* Born and raised in Chicago, he lives in Kalamazoo, Michigan.

EDWARD HOAGLAND has published seven books of essays, including *Heart's Desire;* four novels, including *Seven Rivers*

West; and two travel books, including *Notes from the Century Before.* In 1982, he was elected a member of the American Academy of Arts and Letters. He teaches at Bennington College in Bennington, Vermont.

ALICE HOFFMAN is the author of eleven novels, including *Turtle Moon, Second Nature,* and, most recently, *Practical Magic.* She lives in Massachusetts with her family.

BELL HOOKS is a writer and professor, who speaks widely on issues of race, class, and gender. Her previous books include *Ain't I a Woman, Feminist Theory, Talking Back, Yearning, Breaking Bread: Insurgent Black Intellectual Life* (with Cornel West), *Killing Rage,* and, most recently, the memoir *Bone Black.* She lives in New York City.

CHANG-RAE LEE is the author of *Native Speaker* and a forthcoming novel. He teaches creative writing at the University of Oregon and lives in Eugene, Oregon, with his wife. "The Faintest Echo of Our Language" was his first published piece.

ELIZABETH McCRACKEN is the author of *Here's Your Hat, What's Your Hurry?* and *The Giant's House.* She lives in Massachusetts.

Elizabeth Perowsky died on May 8, 1996, four hours after giving a dance lesson.

WHITNEY OTTO is the author of *How to Make an American Quilt* and *Now You See Her.* Born and raised in California, she currently lives in Portland, Oregon, with her husband, John, their son, Sam, and their dog, Marley.

"Kali died during the time I was working on this piece. She was about twenty years old (we never knew her exact age, since she was a grown cat when we adopted her). We miss her (and her oddball sister in arms, J.B.) terribly."

JAYNE ANNE PHILLIPS is the author of two books of short stories, *Black Tickets* and *Fast Lanes;* and two novels, *Machine Dreams* and *Shelter.* She was born and raised in West Virginia and now lives near Boston with her family.

BOB SHACOCHIS is a novelist, journalist, and educator. He is the author of four books, including *Swimming in the Volcano* and *Domesticity: A Gastronomic Interpretation of Love.* His account of the U.S. military intervention in Haiti, *The Immaculate Invasion,* will be published in 1997.

JANE SMILEY is the author of eight works of fiction, including *The Age of Grief* (which was nominated for a National Book Award), *The Greenlanders, Ordinary Love & Good Will, A Thousand Acres* (which was awarded the Pulitzer Prize), and *Moo.* She lives in Ames, Iowa.

BRENT STAPLES holds a Ph.D. in psychology from The University of Chicago and writes editorials on politics and culture for the *New York Times.* His memoir, *Parallel Time: Growing Up in Black and White,* won the Anisfield-Wolf Book Award in 1995 and was a finalist of the Los Angeles Book Award in 1994. He lives in Brooklyn.

DEBORAH TANNEN is the author of *You Just Don't Understand: Women and Men in Conversation, Talking From 9 to 5,* and

That's Not What I Meant!, among many other books. She is University Professor and Professor of Linguistics at Georgetown University. In addition to her linguistic research and writing, she has published poetry and short stories and has written two plays, one of which, "An Act of Devotion," is included in *The Best American Short Plays: 1993–1994.*

MARION WINIK is heard regularly on National Public Radio's "All Things Considered." She is the author of *Telling,* a collection of essays, and *First Comes Love,* a memoir. She lives in Austin, Texas, with her two sons.

GEOFFREY WOLFF has felt compelled, after almost twenty years, to return here to the scene and memories of his final encounter with his father, events also briefly engaged in *The Duke of Deception,* the memoir/biography of that complex man. Wolff is also the author of *Black Sun,* a biography of expatriate poet Harry Crosby; *A Day at the Beach,* personal essays; and six novels, most recently, *The Age of Consent.* He directs the graduate fiction Program in Writing at the University of California, Irvine.

. . .

SHARON SLOAN FIFFER teaches English and writing at the University of Illinois, Chicago. She is author of *Imagining America,* which was selected as one of the best one hundred books for young adults by the New York City Public Library in 1991. The former co-executive editor of the literary magazine

Other Voices, she has received several honors for her short fiction, including the Illinois Arts Council Award.

STEVE FIFFER is the author of several nonfiction books, including two collaborations with Morris Dees, founder of the Southern Poverty Law Center: *A Season for Justice,* which won the Christopher Award and the Gustavus Myers Award, and *Hate on Trial,* which was selected as a *New York Times* Notable Book of 1993.

The Fiffers recently co-edited *Home: American Writers Remember Rooms of Their Own,* and co-authored *Fifty Ways to Help Your Community: A Handbook for Change.* They live in Evanston, Illinois, with their three children.

ACKNOWLEDGMENTS ·

This book would not have been possible without the contributions of our own family—extended and real: our editor, Sarah Burnes; our literary agent, Gordon Kato; our children, Kate, Nora, and Robert; our mothers, Elaine Fiffer and Nellie Schmidt; and the seventeen wonderful writers whose portraits grace these pages. Thanks to all.